Copyright © 2022 Visual Faith™ Ministry

ISBN: 9798787915044 · Independently published by Visual Faith™ Ministry, Springfield, VA

Visual Faith™ Ministry is the trademark of Visual Faith™ Ministry, LLC.

Layout: Linda Ekong
Cover logo/design: Diane Marra
Typefaces: Alegreya Sans and Archivo Black

VISUAL
FAITH™
MINISTRY

The Movable Adventure

This Bible Study is a stand alone study and also a printed bonus companion piece to the online Movable Adventure videos from Visual Faith™ Ministry.

The Movable Adventure is comprised of over 40 videos that are accessible by purchasing *The Movable Adventure* at visualfaithmin.org/movable. The library of videos is accessed via the website and requires internet access. The Movable Adventure has 4 Pathways. There is a Movable Adventure Companion Journal which gives space for you to take notes, respond, reflect, and meditate on what was heard and what it means for your faith walk.

To purchase The Movable Adventure visit: visualfaithmin.org/movable.

Personal Pathway ...   10 Videos

Is Change Possible?
We do not live static lives. We are dynamic beings, ever-changing for the positive or the negative. This Personal Pathway of Spiritual Transformation is filled with His Word and creative prayer practices that will move you ever closer to the Lord. We begin with a deep dive into the theme verse for this Adventure with a Bible Study on Romans 12:1-2.

Households of Faith Pathway ...   13 Videos

Discover why households matter and the biblical understanding of the household. Explore ways for families on the go to connect together in daily life and how to nurture faith within the household. What is a spiritually vibrant household? Learn how to create a legacy with faith milestones and seasonal celebrations applicable to all life stages.

Community Discipleship Pathway ...   13 Videos

What's Your Next Step?
Exploring faith practices in neighborhoods, classrooms, and in your local church settings. Find out how to create a Hope Table in your neighborhood. Learn about tools for Confirmation instruction, visual faith application for the Lord's Prayer, and Small Group Extensions.

Digital Pathway ...   10 Videos

Following Jesus Online - What's the Shape of your Digital Witness?
Transformational stories about how to use Procreate, Facebook, Instagram, Pinterest, and Zoom as platforms for your digital faith witness. Join a movement of like-minded Christians who want to shine their digital lights in a dark world.

TABLE OF CONTENTS

A Note from the Author

Engaging in intentional Bible study lies at the heart and soul of our spiritual walk. Along with a vibrant prayer life, reading and responding to God's Word will draw you into His presence, ignite relationship with the Lord, and support the growth of a Christian community inside of your life. With those goals in mind, we dive deep into God's Word together.

Getting the most out of this study is the deepest desire of my heart for everyone who picks it up. I pray that you will give yourself over to whatever God's Word has in store for you. Always remember, what strikes passion in your spirit may not be the same as what speaks to the person next to you. That doesn't matter, as the Spirit works as He alone sees fit. Be receptive to God and gracious with others as you share this experience together. If you are working alone through this study, that's okay too. There's still plenty of thinking to be done if you're working by yourself.

This Study comes with *videos* to watch or listen to as well. Those can be found at the **Visual Faith™ Ministry: The Movable Adventure** website at *www.visualfaithmin.org/movablebiblestudy*. You will find that they are listed in the study when it comes time to watch/listen to them. They contain extra information and a few challenges.

Please come into this time in God's Word with your own Bible - whatever version you like the most, (even though most of the readings are printed for you in this book) and something to write/illustrate/doodle with such as colored pencils, markers, highlighters, gel pens ... whatever you like to use to help you remember what you are learning. This is meant to be an experiential learning opportunity.

This study, as it was conceived in my mind, was meant to be four units that could be accomplished in about an hour each. As writing progressed, I found that wasn't even slightly possible. Instead, there are twenty lessons broken into four units. Each lesson could easily take an hour each to work through thoroughly. The more time you spend on each study, and the more digging you do into all the suggested readings, the more you will get out of the experience. I would encourage you to linger, think deeply, and ask questions. Give God a chance to move you, transform you, and draw you ever closer to His side.

God bless your studies!

Carolyn

¹I appeal to you therefore, brothers, by the mercies of God, to present your bodies as a living sacrifice, holy and acceptable to God, which is your spiritual worship. ²Do not be conformed to this world, but be transformed by the renewal of your mind, that by testing you may discern what is the will of God, what is good and acceptable and perfect.
Romans 12:1-2

Thank You

This study could not have happened without the help of several women who have skills I deeply admire. My sincere appreciation goes out to my daughters, Hannah Machado and Bethany Lakies who participated in the teaching videos, Dionne Lovstad-Jones, and Jenny Long, who participated in the podcast, and some very dear and skillful friends, Melody Schwieger, Diana Batema, Diane Marra, Linda Ekong, Denise Miller, Candice Schwark, Pat Maier, Emily Adams, Katie Helmreich, Valerie Matyas, Deborah Rohne, Marsha Baker, Renee Whitener, Karen Bosch, Janet Blocher, and Gayle Thorn. God has surrounded me with strong and generous women who want to see God's Kingdom expand.

Explanation of the Visual Faith Components

Throughout this study you will find various visual faith components.

1. Bible Margins - You can use these to color while meditating on the scripture reading, trace it into your own bible, etc.

2. Creative Writing Scripture Word Art - At the end of each unit there is an image where you can write your favorite verse from the unit. An example is here to the right. You can find additional instructions, sample writing, and additional blank images to copy or use in the "Lingering Over His Word" portion of this book starting on page 123.

3. Sketchnotes - Each of the video files have been sketchnoted by our sketchnote team and follow those lessons in the book. We also have a blank page following the sample sketchnote for you to give it a try. To learn more about sketchnoting you can watch the video provided at *visualfaithmin.org/movablebiblestudy*. These beautiful sketchnotes are in black and white in this book, however we also have the original colored versions of these available at *visualfaithmin.org/movablebiblestudy*.

4. Lingering Over His Word - Denise Miller and Candice Schwark have created some additional visual faith components and accompanying videos. They begin on page 123.

For ease in accessing the Video files in this Bible study, you can visit visualfaithmin.org/movablebiblestudy or use the QR Code to the left with your phone or tablet.

Unit One

... But, Be Transformed

Open with prayer.

Dear Awesome God, Father, Son, and Holy Spirit, we praise and magnify Your name, for You are Lord over all of us. None other compares with Your great majesty. We worship You with all that we are. Holy Spirit, You are welcome here. Inhabit our hearts and minds as we read Your Word and lay ourselves before the truth that lives within the Holy Scriptures. Show each one of us the message You have prepared for us. Attune our ears to Your will and way. Transform our thinking, that we might be in greater agreement with Your heart. This time is of Your making, and we are surrendered to Your work in us. In the name of Jesus we pray. Amen.

Discussion Question:

If you don't know everyone in the group, make sure to take the time and introduce yourselves and share just a little bit about what brings you to the study time. Also, share with the group what you hope to get out of this time in God's Word together.

Take a few moments and write out the words of Romans 12:1–2 on the lines below in your own hand. Open your Bible and transfer the words of the Apostle Paul onto your Bible study pages. **Underline or highlight with color the words that seem the most important.** As you write out the passage, **make note of whatever insights, questions, or comments** you have about these words as you give them close scrutiny. [If you're doing this study with a group, allow plenty of time for the participants to work through this exercise. Then, allow time for sharing and discussion. *If you are the group leader, make special note of any questions that emerge, as these will be valuable talking points.*]

Romans 12:-1–2 (what version? NIV ESV NASB KJV other _____)

_____

_____

_____

_____

_____

The Movable Adventure is all about learning how to cooperate with God as He draws you ever closer to Himself. The passage from Romans in the last exercise speaks directly to that spiritual lifestyle. God is all about the work of transforming your heart and mind so that they are in concert with His will and His way. This is the task of spiritual transformation. As we ponder this transformation, we need to also think about the role that spiritual knowledge plays in this conversation.

Discussion Questions:

Talk about the difference between knowledge and transformation.

- **Knowledge:** facts, information, and skills acquired by a person through experience or education; the theoretical or practical understanding of a subject
- **Transformation:** make a thorough or dramatic change in the form, appearance, or character of

How are these two ideas different when it comes to our faith? Why does Paul use the word *transformed* rather than *trained* or *taught*?

_____

Paul warns us in 1 Corinthians 8:1, "*Knowledge puffs up, but love builds up*". In humanity's first interaction with evil, between Adam and Eve, and Satan, the serpent lies to them, using incorrect knowledge offered by someone who hated God.

Genesis 3:1–8

In Satan's few, brief challenges to what God said to Adam and Eve, he questions God's truthfulness, plants the lie that they wouldn't actually die, and ignites a love for knowledge that would supersede a love for God. Don't get me wrong—I'm all about more knowledge, especially knowledge about God. But when our only goal is gaining more information, we supplant the need to do the deeper and more difficult work of allowing that knowledge to bring about transformation.

As the pinnacle of Creation, Adam and Eve weren't in need of transformation. But in choosing to believe Satan's lies, they find themselves in a new place—outside of God's perfect will for them. False knowledge becomes the enemy. Suddenly, transformation becomes imperative. God is not surprised by any of these events, and in fact, He knew what was going to happen before Creation even began. He already has a plan in place that will bring the ultimate transformation: His people will be transformed from sinners into saints by the blood of His Dear Son, Jesus Christ. And He promises such in Genesis 3:15. But, in that moment of sin, the need for transformation becomes the way forward.

Write out the words of Genesis 3:15. Here we find the first promise of a Messiah.

9

One of the meatiest, most well-studied verses in all of the Bible are the words of Paul in Romans 12:1–2, the theme verses for this spiritual adventure.

¹I appeal to you therefore, brothers, by the mercies of God, to present your bodies as a living sacrifice, holy and acceptable to God, which is your spiritual worship. ²Do not be conformed to this world, but be transformed by the renewal of your mind, that by testing you may discern what is the will of God, what is good and acceptable and perfect.

In these words, Paul instructs us to give ourselves over to the transformational work that takes place by the power of the Holy Spirit, through the gift of His Word and the act of worship. The focus of this study is to examine the pathway of that transformative work. Also, let's agree there will not be a moment in this lifetime where you will have "arrived". This work is a life-long journey, completed in full when Christ returns on the Last Day and our bodies are resurrected to His glorious side. In the meantime, we experience the ongoing transformative work of His hands in our lives through the power and presence of the Holy Spirit. The spiritual word for transformation is sanctification. This means "to be made holy". This work is displayed in our lives when we exhibit more Fruit of the Spirit [love, joy, peace, patience, kindness, goodness, faithfulness, self-control – see Galatians 5:22–23], rich prayer life, reliance upon God for all things, service to others etc.

Before we dive into the text, one detail needs to be addressed: the word *therefore* in verse 1. [*I appeal to you therefore,*] Whenever we see that word, we need to look back a few verses to see what the writer is calling us to examine. In this case, it is the verses immediately before the passage of our study and actually the first eleven chapters of Romans. Read these verses and attach them to Romans 12:1–2.

Romans 11:33–12:2 *(ESV)*

³³Oh, the depth of the riches and wisdom and knowledge of God! How unsearchable are his judgments and how inscrutable his ways! ³⁴"For who has known the mind of the Lord, or who has been his counselor?" ³⁵"Or who has given a gift to him that he might be repaid?" ³⁶For from him and through him and to him are all things. To him be glory forever. Amen. ¹I appeal to you therefore, brothers, by the mercies of God, to present your bodies as a living sacrifice, holy and acceptable to God, which is your spiritual worship. ²Do not be conformed to this world, but be transformed by the renewal of your mind, that by testing you may discern what is the will of God, what is good and acceptable and perfect.

Discussion Question:

How does the *therefore* impact your reading of 12:1–2?

_____

_____

_____

_____

_____

So, let's look at this rich and provocative verse, giving attention to the details.

*¹I appeal to you therefore, brothers, by the **mercies of God**, to **present your bodies** as a living sacrifice, holy and acceptable to God, which is your **spiritual worship**. ²**Do not be conformed** to this world, but **be transformed** by **the renewal of your mind**, that by **testing** you may discern what is the will of God, what is good and acceptable and perfect.*

Mercies of God – God is first – God goes first ➡ 1ˢᵗ Commandment (see Exodus 20)

- In all things (except sin) God goes first. As soon as we're aligned with that way of thinking, we are relying on God rather than ourselves. This is a must, for we are helpless to accomplish this work without Him.

- If one ever loses sight of God's mercies, Paul's exhortations in Romans 12 run the danger of becoming legalistic or moralistic. This never enhances our faith.

- In 2021, one way we lose sight of God's mercies is a prevailing attitude coined "moral deism". Christian Smith and Melissa Lundquist Denton explain the serious issues with these ideas about God.

  1. A God exists who created and orders the world and watches over human life on earth.

  2. God wants people to be good, nice, and fair to each other, as taught in the Bible and by most world religions.

  3. The central goal of life is to be happy and to feel good about oneself.

  4. God does not need to be particularly involved in one's life except when God is needed to resolve a problem.

  5. Good people go to heaven when they die.

  6. Jesus is more of a mascot than a Deity.

Soul Searching: The Religious and Spiritual Lives of American Teenagers
© 2009 Christian Smith/Melissa Lundquist Denton Oxford University Press

Insights – Questions – Comments – Surprises – Words You Highlighted

_____

_____

_____

_____

_____

_____

Close with prayer.

Unit One

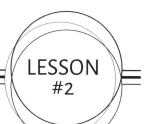

Moral Deism

 **Open with prayer.**

Gracious Heavenly Father, we are always grateful to gather under Your Word. Holy Spirit, be welcome here to speak into our hearts and minds. Enliven our spirits as we discuss what You have for us today and challenge our thinking and actions by the direction of your message for us. We long to be ever shaped and transformed by Your hand and surrender to that good work in us today. In the name of Jesus we pray. Amen.

Watch video #1 "The Word Speaks #1" that accompanies this lesson at Visual Faith™ Ministry: Movable Adventure Bible Study visualfaithmin.org/movablebiblestudy

[Since the video is 45 minutes long, it will carry the majority of your study time for this lesson. If you wish to skip the video, simply move onto the next lesson after you've discussed the question accompanying this lesson. After the video is completed, discuss the question below.]

Discussion Questions:

Have you seen any of these attitudes in the people around you or perhaps in your own thinking? Do you agree with Smith and Lundquist Denton that many in our culture are embracing these ideas about God?

Close with prayer.

My Sketchnotes

Unit One

The Worship Lifestyle

Open with prayer.

Dear Lord God, Father, Son, and Holy Spirit. Enliven and enlighten us with Your truth and grace through the study of Your Word. Help us to see where You have worked in our lives in the past, and hand over control so that You can do the same in the future. May we always see Your will at work, and teach us to embrace Your movement through our lives. In Jesus' name we pray. Amen.

¹I appeal to you therefore, brothers, by the mercies of God, to present your bodies as a living sacrifice, holy and acceptable to God, which is your spiritual worship. ²Do not be conformed to this world, but be transformed by the renewal of your mind, that by testing you may discern what is the will of God, what is good and acceptable and perfect. Romans 12:1–2 (ESV)

Discussion Questions:

As we ponder the transformative nature of walking through this life with Jesus as Lord, what kinds of spiritual transformations have already taken place in your life? How are you spiritually different today than you were in the past?

_____

_____

_____

_____

_____

In this lesson, we will examine the pathway of transformation as laid out for us by Paul in Romans 12. There are several admonitions Paul spells out that we do well to understand so that there is more room for them in our lives.

Present your bodies 3ʳᵈ Commandment

o Paul's admonition is unlike the Old Testament sacrifice where you gave your lamb (or pigeon, or ram, or goat ...) and walked away. [See Leviticus 9 for further information on the sacrificial system.] We cannot disparage this system, as it is one of God's making. But when Jesus comes into the picture in the New Testament, the need for those sacrifices disappears, as He is the final and perfect sacrifice for our sins. So Paul presents a New Testament twist on the practice of making a sacrifice. If you've "presented your body", rather than a dead animal, *you cannot walk away*. This is about an internal action that naturally leads us to the concept of what it means to live a worship lifestyle.

Extra Information

Three adjectives modify the kind of sacrifice under consideration: "living, holy, [and] well-pleasing".

1. Paul uses *life/living* in both the more common physical sense, as well as with the theological meaning of life in relationship with God through Christ. It refers to the nature of the sacrifice itself: one that does not die as it is offered but goes on living. If so, the oxymoronic nature of a "living" sacrifice is striking.

The next two adjectives clearly have an OT background in the formal worship God prescribed for his sanctuary.

2. *Holy*, carries the OT notion of "set apart." Thus it entails "being dedicated or consecrated to the service of God". But as a modifier for "sacrifice", Paul surely intends a shading over into the sense *holy = pure, perfect*. Thus "holy" describes a sacrifice that has been sanctified, purified, and cleansed.

3. The sacrifice is *well-pleasing to God*. One translation option would be to attach "to God" to the "sacrifice" in a manner which then encompasses all three adjectives: "a sacrifice to God that is living, holy, and well-pleasing." To be well-pleasing to/before God is LXX phraseology for people who live and walk by faith.

Middendorf, M. P. ©2016. *Romans 9–16*. (pp. 1214–1216). Saint Louis, MO: CPH.

Discussion Questions:

Unpack the information above. (Some of this is couched in fairly heavy theological language. Give yourself a break if it's hard to understand, and go slowly.) Is there anything that is unclear? How does this information inform your understanding of what it means to "present your body as a living sacrifice"?

Talk about the difference between the Old Testament way of sacrifice and Paul's "updated" version. How does that impact your idea of presenting yourself as a living sacrifice?

Spiritual Worship – What is that? 3rd Commandment (see Exodus 20)

o   Watch/Listen to *The Heart of Worship by Matt Redman. You can find it on YouTube. Search for "The Heart of Worship, Matt Redman, Story" or visit visualfaithmin.org/movablebiblestudy to find the link.*

o   As theologian, Martin Franzmann, writes in his Romans Commentary: "The new worship is inspired, not imposed *on* man but created *in* man by the God who gives life to the dead." "Through the mercies of God" (12:1), such worship is, in fact, the only 'reasonable,' appropriate, and proper response."

Discussion Questions:

Redman wrote this song as a teenage worship leader. Even then, he became aware through the teaching of his pastor, that he was worshiping the experience of being a worship leader/ song writer, rather than God. This realization caused him to put away all music during worship for a time. When the need to worship the music was gone, this was the song that God gave to the church. Does this story create a response in you? What might you be worshiping instead of God? It's a difficult question, but one that needs to be revisited frequently.

Do NOT conform to the world 4th – 10th Commandments (see Exodus 20)

Discussion Questions:

This is about ALL aspects of our daily living with the people around us. How does serving your neighbor look like staying clear of conforming to the ways of the world? This question isn't as easy as it may seem at first. What are some of the complications that arise for you as you seek to live well with your neighbors? (A first step might be to define exactly who is your neighbor. See Luke 10:25–37)

Close with prayer.

Unit One

Conformed or Transformed?

Open with prayer.

Awesome God, because of Your great love, You have created us to be Your children. We know that we face struggles and challenges because of the power of sin in the world. But we also know that You never send us out alone. Inspire in us an even greater understanding of who You are and how You provide the strength that we must have to live our faith out loud. In the name of Jesus we pray. Amen.

Discussion Questions:

What challenges have you faced during the last few days/weeks regarding the ongoing battle every Christian must face: how to avoid conforming to the world around us? How did you win out or lose out to those battles?

In this lesson, we are going to discuss the difference between conforming and being transformed.

Be transformed – Seeking God for transformation → (1st Commandment)

Conformed	Transformed
Listen to and follow the flesh	Let God lead my life
Fear of man	Fear of God
Thinking shaped by news/social media	Life shaped by the Word
Time spent in Entertainment/Social Media	Time in prayer
Live as you please	Live consistently with the Word
Time squandered	Time redeemed
Follow your own will	Seek God's will and obey

Extra Information

The two imperatives translated as "be conformed" and "be transformed" have different verbal roots, but they "are more or less synonymous in Greek," and the wordplay in English is effective. The following distinction between the two in Greek has often been asserted: the first, indicates an outward conforming in contrast to the inward transformation of the second. A separation of the inner from the outer is unwise in regard to both. Resisting conformity is *not* simply outward since even Paul openly admits that sin still "is dwelling in me ... that is, in my flesh". Furthermore, the transformation *of bodies* into a living sacrifice surely exhibits itself in outward manifestations.

Be "transformed" is most likely passive and means to resist *being conformed* by outward pressures. In any case, Origen describes those who conform as follows: "If there are those who love this present life and the things which are in the world, they are taken up with the form of the present age and pay no attention to what is not seen."

Both imperatives are also *present tense*. The general precepts which convey an ongoing activity, rather than something fulfilled in a single event. Thus Paul's commands reflect *an ongoing reality which calls for continual and necessary vigilance on the part of believers.*

Middendorf, M. P. (2016). *Romans 9–16.* (pp. 1219–1223). Saint Louis, MO: CPH.

Discussion Questions:

While God is the One doing the transforming, we are most certainly involved. Which topics in the two columns do you relate to personally – on both sides of the table? What actions or activities would you need help to add (or subtract) from your life?

Renewal of the Mind

Recognize the fact that our minds are the source of our troubles. We are able to come up with an infinite number of evil things. But God is able (and willing) to help us tame our minds and all we have to do is step out of the way. One of our most incredible tools can be found in **2 Corinthians 10:4–5** *(ESV)*.

⁴For the weapons of our warfare are not of the flesh but have divine power to destroy strongholds. ⁵We destroy arguments and every lofty opinion raised against the knowledge of God, and take every thought captive to obey Christ.

Discussion Questions:

What is "renewal of the mind" to you? How does it happen? What are you putting into your mind? The things of God or the things of this world? What is coming out of your mouth? (For whatever you put in, you will spew out.)

Test (how well I'm accomplishing) the will of God

- o The purpose of all of it – living inside of God's perfect will.
- o Discerning His will means we learn how to LISTEN and then SUBMIT to His way.

Discussion Questions:

How well are you doing when it comes to living inside of God's perfect will? Where are you successful and where do you struggle?

Close with prayer.

Unit One

Practical Application

Open with prayer. - Psalm 27 *(ESV)*
Read the Psalm aloud as your prayer. Circle any words or phrases that stand out. When the psalm has been read, take 3 minutes of silence to ponder those words.

¹*The Lord is my light and my salvation; whom shall I fear?*

The Lord is the stronghold of my life; of whom shall I be afraid?

²*When evildoers assail me to eat up my flesh, my adversaries and foes, it is they who stumble and fall.*

³*Though an army encamp against me, my heart shall not fear; though war arise against me, yet I will be confident.*

⁴*One thing have I asked of the Lord, that will I seek after: that I may dwell in the house of the Lord all the days of my life, to gaze upon the beauty of the Lord and to inquire in his temple.*

⁵*For he will hide me in his shelter in the day of trouble; he will conceal me under the cover of his tent; he will lift me high upon a rock.*

⁶*And now my head shall be lifted up above my enemies all around me, and I will offer in his tent sacrifices with shouts of joy; I will sing and make melody to the Lord.*

⁷*Hear, O Lord, when I cry aloud; be gracious to me and answer me!*

⁸*You have said, "Seek my face." My heart says to you, "Your face, Lord, do I seek."*

⁹*Hide not your face from me. Turn not your servant away in anger, O you who have been my help. Cast me not off; forsake me not, O God of my salvation!*

¹⁰*For my father and my mother have forsaken me, but the Lord will take me in.*

¹¹*Teach me your way, O Lord, and lead me on a level path because of my enemies.*

¹²*Give me not up to the will of my adversaries; for false witnesses have risen against me, and they breathe out violence.*

¹³*I believe that I shall look upon the goodness of the Lord in the land of the living!*

¹⁴*Wait for the Lord; be strong, and let your heart take courage; wait for the Lord!*

Watch video #2 "The Word Speaks #2" that accompanies this lesson at Visual Faith™ Ministry: Movable Adventure Bible Study
visualfaithmin.org/movablebiblestudy

Re-evaluate: Re-examine your hand-written version of Romans 12:1–2 on page 7. How has your understanding changed or grown? How does this impact your spiritual transformation and your walk with Jesus?

As we consider what it means to be transformed by the Lord, let's take time to hear what He has to say about us. What does He know and how does He use that information? Use this passage for personal meditation or Lectio Divina. If you would like more information on the practice of Lectio Divina, we demonstrate it on page 49 in Unit 2 Lesson 4. A video is also available.

Psalm 139:1–6, 23–24 *(ESV)*

¹O Lord, you have searched me and known me!

²You know when I sit down and when I rise up; you discern my thoughts from afar.

³You search out my path and my lying down and are acquainted with all my ways.

⁴Even before a word is on my tongue, behold, O Lord, you know it altogether.

⁵You hem me in, behind and before, and lay your hand upon me.

⁶Such knowledge is too wonderful for me; it is high; I cannot attain it.

²³Search me, O God, and know my heart! Try me and know my thoughts!

²⁴And see if there be any grievous way in me, and lead me in the way everlasting!

What words jump out for you? What strikes at your heart today? Write or illustrate what you are learning below. Or doodle around "How God Knows Me" on the next page.

How God Knows Me

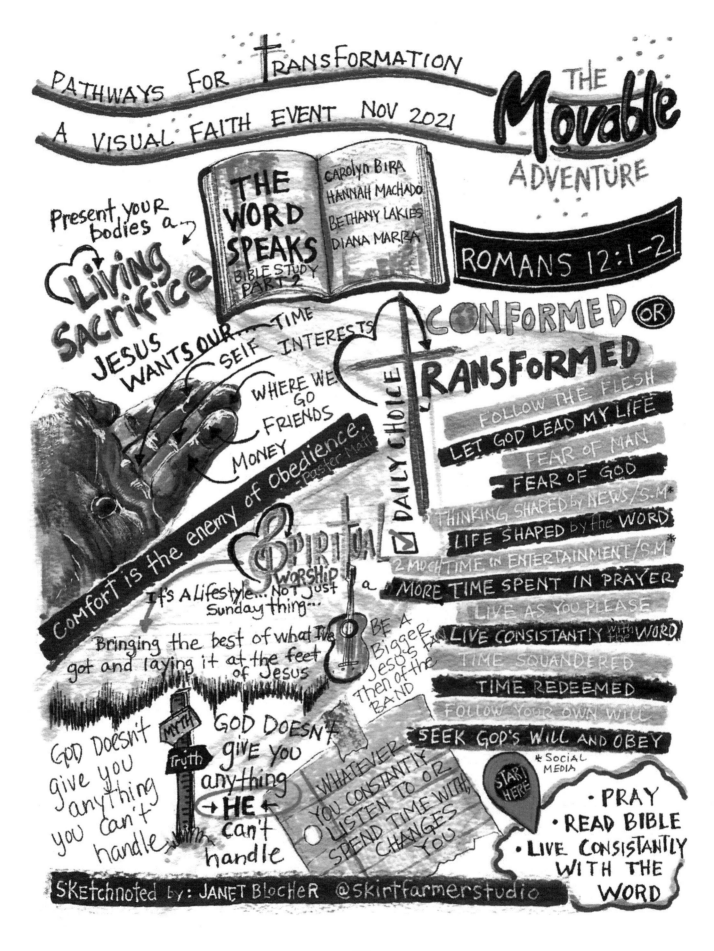

My Sketchnotes

Favorite Scripture Verse from Unit 1

Unit Two

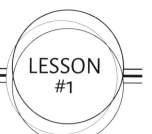

A Rocky Start

Open with Prayer.

Gracious Lord God, Father, Son, and Holy Spirit. To You alone belongs all glory, honor, and praise. Thank You for time in your Word; time spent with You. Holy Spirit, open our hearts and minds to Your leading. Illuminate Your Word so that the truths we find on these pages fills us with hope, peace, understanding, and insight. Thank You for the precious gift. We open it with expectation and excitement as you pour out what You have prepared for us. Thank You for these tremendous blessings. In Jesus' name we pray. Amen.

We come to the faith in a myriad of ways. Some at the feet of faithful parents, some through the trials of life as they search for God, and some even come through a miraculous visitation of the Lord into their lives. What is your story? How did the Lord bring you to know His story of saving grace? How have you responded to that story? If you're working through this study with a group, **briefly share the highlights** of your story with them.

Watch video #3 "Digital Missioner - Instagram" that accompanies this lesson at Visual Faith™ Ministry: Movable Adventure Bible Study
visualfaithmin.org/movablebiblestudy
In this video, three women share their own personal faith journeys, and their stories are quite compelling.

We've embarked on a journey together, exploring the idea of spiritual transformation. This adventure has been dubbed "Movable" because we all know that we are ever shifting creatures. Sometimes we shift in a positive direction, and sometimes not so positive. Regardless, we are invited by the Lord to give our lives over to the Holy Spirit's work of spiritual transformation. As always, we look to God's Word for our pathway. One of the most well-known of our spiritual forefathers is Moses, leader of God's people for 40 years. His story is well documented and most certainly displays how God changes our lives. This lesson focuses on the first 40 years of Moses' life. This particular lesson contains a great deal of historical information. While much of it is not in the Bible, we can certainly avail ourselves of a little archeology and ancient history.

Exodus 2:1–10 – Read this aloud *(ESV)*

¹*Now a man from the house of Levi went and took as his wife a Levite woman.* ²*The woman conceived and bore a son, and when she saw that he was a fine child, she hid him three months.* ³*When she could hide him no longer, she took for him a basket made of bulrushes and daubed it with bitumen and pitch. She put the child in it and placed it among the reeds by the riverbank.* ⁴*And his sister stood at a distance to know what would be done to him.* ⁵*Now the daughter of Pharaoh came down to bathe at the river, while her young women walked beside the river. She saw the basket among the reeds and sent her servant woman, and she took it.* ⁶*When she opened it, she saw the child, and behold, the baby was crying. She took pity on him and said, "This is one of the Hebrews' children."* ⁷*Then his sister said to Pharaoh's daughter, "Shall I go and call you a nurse from the Hebrew women to nurse the child for you?"* ⁸*And Pharaoh's daughter said to her, "Go." So the girl went and called the child's mother.* ⁹*And Pharaoh's daughter said to her, "Take this child away and nurse him for me, and I will give you your wages." So the woman took the child and nursed him.* ¹⁰*When the child grew older, she brought him to Pharaoh's daughter, and he became her son. She named him Moses, "Because," she said, "I drew him out of the water."*

Discussion Questions:

What are your initial reactions to this reading? What questions emerge? What comments would you make to the participants in this story of rescue for a small baby?

Before God can send a "deliverer" to His people, to free them from their bondage to the Egyptians, He must first deliver Moses from the hands of the Pharaoh who would kill him simply for being born a male at the wrong time in history. This story of Moses' rescue from being murdered by drowning in the Nile is often recounted. First, let's look at the Pharaoh.

This Pharaoh is a man who ruthlessly is willing to kill anyone (including babies) if they pose a threat. He saw those baby boys as future soldiers in a Hebrew army making them fair game for extermination before that could happen. The "Pharaoh's daughter" was also an interesting position to hold. She was most likely one of possibly dozens of daughters. The pharaohs were certainly not monogamous, and daughters were quite useful in making political alliances, so having numerous children was an asset. This woman was most likely unmarried at this point and free as the pharaoh's daughter to do as she wished, including adopting a Hebrew baby boy. Because of her place as one of many daughters we might consider the possibility that Moses had very little to do with the reigning Pharaoh. The king may not have known Moses as he grew up.

> "Pharaoh" is Egyptian for "big house" so that reference to the pharaoh in Exodus is somewhat like using the term "the White House" in modern times, as in "The White House said today that no new legislation would be proposed." It refers generally to the government and national leader, but only from the point of view of the office and not the man. In Exodus, Moses used "Pharaoh" more often than his other generic term for the same person, "king of Egypt," but interchanged the two terms without any obvious intentional pattern.
>
> Stuart, D. K. ©2006. *Exodus* (Vol. 2). Nashville: Broadman & Holman Publishers.

Who Is Moses?

His Hebrew Parents

- Brave parents — both Levites by lineage
  - Mother — Jochebed (the one who contrived and carried out the risky plan)
  - Father — Amram
- Moses is a Levite BEFORE that was important — the covenant lifestyle with God had not yet been established. That covenant, which was started with Adam and Eve in Genesis 3, and reaffirmed with Abraham in Exodus 15, is established firmly later in Exodus.
- Rabbinic tradition says Jochebed named him *Tobiah* — ['Tov' = *it is good*] If this is indeed the name his mother gave him, we see that she had hope and faith in God for Moses' [Tobiah's] future.

> **A note about Rabbinic Tradition:** For the Christian, rabbinic tradition is *not* on the same authoritative level as Scriptures. But there is much to be gained in terms of understanding the lives of God's people who are living in a culture that is drastically different from what we experience today. Insights from what are known as *extra-biblical* resources are considered for no reason other than that. These "facts" are not found in the Bible and as such, not 100% reliable. They are historical details meant only to provide an understanding of the culture and social atmosphere Moses experienced.

Pharaoh's Daughter?

- Pharaoh Amenhotep II, was (possibly) the Pharaoh of the Exodus.
- OR she could have been one of a dozen Egyptian princesses — no one of special notice
- Amenhotep's great-aunt was the Egyptian princess called Hatshepsut. This princess was daughter of a pharaoh and wife of a pharaoh
- Hatshepsut only produced a single female heir, and apparently could not have any more children (this may explain her desire to adopt a son).
- Her husband and half-brother, later to become Pharaoh Tuthmose II, produced a male heir through another wife.
- This heir, Tuthmose III, began to reign at the age of 2, though due to his age, Hatshepsut took control as co-regent and she made herself a fully-fledged pharaoh over Egypt.
- This *could* have been the same princess that rescued and raised Moses. That is only speculation.
- Pharaoh's daughter named him Moses
  - *Moses* = "one who draws out" — a play on taking him from the river and a foreshadow of his future as rescuer of God's people, drawing them out of Egypt
    - Moseh or Mashah — "to beget a son" — "to draw out"
    - She probably knew he was a Hebrew because he was most likely circumcised, so her mercy was intentionally defiant of the Pharaoh's call to have all infant males killed

Watch video #4 "A Rocky Start" that accompanies this lesson at Visual Faith™ Ministry: Movable Adventure Bible Study visualfaithmin.org/movablebiblestudy

Close with prayer.

If you have time, use the last page of this lesson to engage in a Prayer Journaling practice that will give you time to pray for and praise God for your own family. Using the *stained-glass prayer practice* on the next page, raise up your family before the Lord today. Write each of their names in the spaces provided and pray for their particular needs as you color or decorate the space that holds their name. Choose one person to close the group time with a short prayer at the end of this silent (and creative) prayer.

P RAISE
R EPENT
A SK
Y IELD

the WORD speaks

PSALM 2.
...d's Confidence in God, H...
A Psalm of David
THE LORD is "my she...
shall not want.
2 He maketh me to lie ...
green pastures; 'he lea...
...side the 'still waters
'He 'restoreth my
...th me in ...

a rocky START

Study Unit 2   # 1

• Carolyn Bira • Dionne Lovstad Jones •
• Jenny Long •

We are ALL on a
⚓ FAITH JOURNEY

Dionne
• Visual Faith Ministries leader
• a Faith Journey guided by parents
• sometimes bumpy/roller coaster

Jenny
• born into family always in church
• dark time/rebelled
• joined Praise Band – husband shared Jesus

Carolyn
• baptized Catholic
• age 2 family became Lutheran
• always loved church

MOSES' Faith Journey
• very detailed
• transparent abt. Moses' struggles
• born a Levite
• spiritual transformation

STRONG WOMEN
in Moses' Life

• MIDWIFE
• MOTHER — crafty (basket) — courage
• SISTER — quick thinking
• PHARAOH'S DAUGHTER
  └ rescued/adopted him
  └ named him "MOSES" (to draw out)

PHARAOH – the Egyptian government, as well as the ruler

→ KILL   the Hebrew baby boys

what is *your* FAITH JOURNEY?

RABBINIC TRADITION ○ ○

adds depth to our understanding

Moses' Hebrew name "TOBIAH" (it is good)

Sketchnote by Karen Bosch @karlyb

My Sketchnotes

Unit Two

It's an Ark

Open with Prayer:

Dear Lord God, Father, Son, and Holy Spirit. In Your great kindness You have drawn us into this time of Bible study. We invite You to be present with us as we open Your Word and take in whatever You have for us today. Fill us with insight, inspiration, and encouragement as the story of Moses continues to unfold in our hearts and imaginations. Thank You for preserving Your Word in all of its Truth and Power so that we can have this open doorway into Your heart and Your will for us. In Jesus' name we pray. Amen.

Moses as "TYPE" of Christ

[Type of Christ = In the Old Testament, there are several times when people display something that will take place during the life of Jesus Christ. These instances are a foreshadowing of what is to come in God's big story of our salvation.]

- Moses was born under Pharaoh's threat of death to newborn sons
- Jesus was born under Herod's threat of death to newborn sons

Discussion Question:

Are there other Old Testament stories you can remember that might also bear the mark of pointing to Jesus or reminding us of His story? Brainstorm some of those stories together. Write the names of the people involved or just a reminder of the details. One has been done for you to get you started.

Name or Situation	Event or plot
Isaac	Carries wood for the sacrifice (Gen. 22)

Exodus 2:1–10 *(ESV)*

¹Now a man from the house of Levi went and took as his wife a Levite woman. ²The woman conceived and bore a son, and when she saw that he was a fine child, she hid him three months. ³When she could hide him no longer, she took for him a basket made of bulrushes and daubed it with bitumen and pitch. She put the child in it and placed it among the reeds by the riverbank. ⁴And his sister stood at a distance to know what would be done to him. ⁵Now the daughter of Pharaoh came down to bathe at the river, while her young women walked beside the river. She saw the basket among the reeds and sent her servant woman, and she took it. ⁶When she opened it, she saw the child, and behold, the baby was crying. She took pity on him and said, "This is one of the Hebrews' children." ⁷Then his sister said to Pharaoh's daughter, "Shall I go and call you a nurse from the Hebrew women to nurse the child for you?" ⁸And Pharaoh's daughter said to her, "Go." So the girl went and called the child's mother. ⁹And Pharaoh's daughter said to her, "Take this child away and nurse him for me, and I will give you your wages." So the woman took the child and nursed him. ¹⁰When the child grew older, she brought him to Pharaoh's daughter, and he became her son. She named him Moses, "Because," she said, "I drew him out of the water."

Moses' Older Sister, Miriam plays into his story:

Miriam's placement by the river was also quite purposeful. She was probably between the ages of 6–12 and quite capable of keeping watch over Moses during his time in the reeds. We should not suppose that Moses' mother simply let him float down the river and hoped that he would be okay. He was probably placed in that basket (the actual word is "ark" in the Hebrew) and hidden in the reeds. His discovery by the Egyptians would have occurred during the daylight hours had he been kept at home. So at night he was probably brought back into the home and then placed there again in the morning. His mother could head down to the river to nurse him during the day when necessary. His discovery by Pharaoh's daughter makes those daytime ark rides unnecessary, and his life is spared. That Jochebed (Moses' birthmother) gets paid to take care of him is yet another time when God's sense of irony and humor comes alive.

Well-preserved Egyptian basket (c. 1480 B.C.), probably comparable to the one described as carrying Moses. Rogers Fund 1936. Public Domain

Moses' ARK – Tebah (tay-baw)

תֵּבַב *a box, chest—ark (26), basket (2)*

- Translated "basket" in the NIV – not a particularly good translation choice

- The only other uses of this word in the Old Testament are found in the story of Noah and the Ark of the Covenant. The readers/hearers of the story would have immediately made an association with Noah being saved from the flood waters by the Ark.

- Made of papyrus, as was most of the furniture of the day, since lumber would have been in short supply for the Hebrews

- Moses was put into the Ark at 3 months – the age at which keeping an infant quiet becomes difficult.

- He was NOT abandoned to his fate – this was a hiding place only

What we are privileged to witness here is that God's plan will always win out, no matter the obstacles. Pharaoh's desire to see all of the baby boys killed was not an issue for God. He overcame that order by placing the unwillingness to commit these murders into the hearts of the midwives and moving Pharaoh's daughter to instantly want to adopt Moses. God's plan for delivering His people moves forward despite us.

Discussion Questions:

Fortunately, few of us have had to make a choice between two evils in order to keep our infants alive. What kind of trust would it take in God's ability to protect your child such that you would put your baby into a papyrus ark and place them in the Nile River?

As Christians, we simply must rely on the sovereignty of God. That means we believe that He knows all and has all things in His hands. Was the outcome of the decision to put Moses in the papyrus ark and hide him among the reeds miraculous or good luck? Is there any such thing as good luck? Does this story have anything to do with the Sovereignty of God?

How has God taken care of you in miraculous ways? If you can't think of any, think harder.

Watch video #5 "It's an Ark" that accompanies this lesson at
Visual Faith™ Ministry: Movable Adventure Bible Study
visualfaithmin.org/movablebiblestudy

Close with prayer.

the WORD speaks

PSALM 2.
...'s Confidence in God, 23.
A Psalm of David
THE LORD is *my shep
shall not want.
2 He maketh me to lie i
green pastures: *he lea
...side the *still waters
...He restoreth my
...me in ...

it's an ARK

STUDY UNIT 2 #2

STUDY UNIT 2 #2

• Carolyn Bira • Dionne Lovstad Jones •
• Jenny Long •

How has God cared for you in MIRACULOUS WAYS?

MOSES' INFANCY

🍀 Good Luck   or Miraculous ?

Happened by GOD'S PLAN

Moses as a "CHRIST TYPE"
foreshadows
baby boys being killed

Jenny
• adopted 3 daughters abandoned at birth
• not coincidence
GOD incidence

Dionne
• takes more faith to believe it is "LUCK"
• God's DESIGN is revealed
BIT ~ ~by~ BIT

BASKET = Hebrew Word: ARK CHEST
(like Noah & Ark of Covenant)

a word of RESCUE ⟨Rescued / Rescuer

• used environment
• covered in pitch
• holds something SPECIAL
• STRONG
• HIDDEN - not floating / only during day

Moses' Mom didn't have Hob by Lobby

Carolyn
• God is SOVEREIGN
Your life DOES NOT
happen by COINCIDENCE !

Sketchnote by Karen Bosch @karlyb

My Sketchnotes

Unit Two

We All Mess Up

Open with prayer. Read Psalm 90 aloud. It is the only Psalm accredited to Moses.

Discussion Questions:

This lesson will deal with Moses' actions that result in a murder. He forever changes his trajectory into the future with a rash action. Have you experienced something that life-changing on your own path, or been the one who suffered the consequences of someone else's choices? How have you dealt with that, for yourself or with them?

Exodus 2:11–25 *(ESV)*

[11]*One day, when Moses had grown up, he went out to his people and looked on their burdens, and he saw an Egyptian beating a Hebrew, one of his people.* [12]*He looked this way and that, and seeing no one, he struck down the Egyptian and hid him in the sand.* [13]*When he went out the next day, behold, two Hebrews were struggling together. And he said to the man in the wrong, "Why do you strike your companion?"* [14]*He answered, "Who made you a prince and a judge over us? Do you mean to kill me as you killed the Egyptian?" Then Moses was afraid, and thought, "Surely the thing is known."* [15]*When Pharaoh heard of it, he sought to kill Moses. But Moses fled from Pharaoh and stayed in the land of Midian. And he sat down by a well.* [16]*Now the priest of Midian had seven daughters, and they came and drew water and filled the troughs to water their father's flock.* [17]*The shepherds came and drove them away, but Moses stood up and saved them, and watered their flock.* [18]*When they came home to their father Reuel, he said, "How is it that you have come home so soon today?"* [19]*They said, "An Egyptian delivered us out of the hand of the shepherds and even drew water for us and watered the flock."* [20]*He said to his daughters, "Then where is he? Why have you left the man? Call him, that he may eat bread."* [21]*And Moses was content to dwell with the man, and he gave Moses his daughter Zipporah.* [22]*She gave birth to a son, and he called his name Gershom, for he said, "I have been a sojourner in a foreign land."* [23]*During those many days the king of Egypt died, and the people of Israel groaned because of their slavery and cried out for help. Their cry for rescue from slavery came up to God.* [24]*And God heard their groaning, and God remembered his covenant with Abraham, with Isaac, and with Jacob.* [25]*God saw the people of Israel—and God knew.*

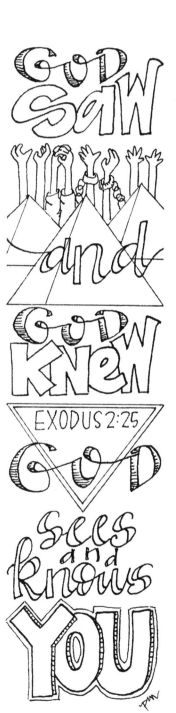

GOD SAW and GOD KNEW
EXODUS 2:25
GOD Sees and knows YOU

Story Details

- Approximately 36 years later—that jump from one significant event to another was (is) a common biographical tool—see the life of Jesus, we know only one story from His childhood!

- Moses goes from being a prince to being a criminal.

- Although Moses identifies with the Hebrews, by killing the Egyptian slave master, Moses fails miserably as a potential future leader of the Jews:

  o Acted alone

  o Done in secret

  o Relied upon his own strength and wisdom

  } *Moses displayed some "princely" arrogance*

Stephen retells this story in Acts 7:23–29 *(ESV)*

[23]*"When he was forty years old, it came into his heart to visit his brothers, the children of Israel.* [24] *And seeing one of them being wronged, he defended the oppressed man and avenged him by striking down the Egyptian.* [25] *He supposed that his brothers would understand that God was giving them salvation by his hand, but they did not understand.* [26] *And on the following day he appeared to them as they were quarreling and tried to reconcile them, saying, 'Men, you are brothers. Why do you wrong each other?'* [27] *But the man who was wronging his neighbor thrust him aside, saying, 'Who made you a ruler and a judge over us?* [28] *Do you want to kill me as you killed the Egyptian yesterday?'* [29] *At this retort Moses fled and became an exile in the land of Midian, where he became the father of two sons.*

- God uses this event to get Moses out of Egypt and into his new training ground, the desert.

- He also picks up a new family. He sits down at a well in Midian, and begins a new life at 40.

Hebrews 11:23–26 *(ESV)*

[23]*By faith Moses, when he was born, was hidden for three months by his parents, because they saw that the child was beautiful, and they were not afraid of the king's edict.* [24]*By faith Moses, when he was grown up, refused to be called the son of Pharaoh's daughter,* [25]*choosing rather to be mistreated with the people of God than to enjoy the fleeting pleasures of sin.* [26]*He considered the reproach of Christ greater wealth than the treasures of Egypt, for he was looking to the reward.*

Discussion Questions:

How does God deal with us when we have done something that seems irreparable? Do the consequences disappear? Are we forgiven? Are you able to forgive yourself? Are you willing to forgive someone who has hurt you? These can be difficult questions. Be as honest as you can. *[For some examples, see Luke 15:11–24, John 8:1–11, 2 Samuel 11:1–12:25, Acts 9:1–19]*

The Bible doesn't withhold the grim facts about the heroes of the faith. Samson (Judges 16) was a womanizer and a bit of a fool; David was an adulterer and a murder (2 Samuel 11); Abraham lied about the fact that Sarah was his wife (Genesis 20:1–2); and Moses murdered a man in cold blood. God's "heroes" are so very human: sinful, confused, and often just completely wrong.

As the story unfolds, Moses' dramatic rescue from Pharaoh's extermination plan as an infant is just the beginning of a big life. At this point in his story, we find Moses at about the age of 40. He has been raised as a prince but still identifies with his own people. He knows that he is a Hebrew and sees their plight. Upon witnessing the beating of a Hebrew he decides to become the deliverer. Note that God has not yet called him into that role. He's making this up as he goes along. That is indeed the future that God has for him, but he is moving ahead of God's timing. In his righteous anger over this beating, he goes too far and commits a murder. The text would indicate that it is probably premeditated. *"He looked this way and that"* implies some forethought. What he probably had not expected was that his own people would not appreciate his actions. Should the murder be discovered, they would all suffer the consequences. Moses is forced to flee both from the Pharaoh and from his own people. God uses this incident to move Moses into the next phase of his training as a national leader. He heads into the desert to live the quiet life of a shepherd.

God clearly has a plan for Moses, and it will not be thwarted. God uses this terrible act of violence to move Moses into the next phase of his training. Up to this point, Moses' interaction with God has been fairly limited, at least as far as Moses is concerned. We don't have any indication that he knows God very well at all. But that doesn't stop God, for His plans are not dependent on our knowledge of what He's doing or our need to "help" Him. What we see in this story is God's ability to move His plans forward without our help while involving us at the deepest level.

Moses is now on the run from both the Egyptians and the Hebrews. He finds himself in Midian and meets the family of Reuel (also known as Jethro). This is an important meeting for Moses as these people become his new family. He marries the daughter of Reuel, Zipporah and has a son, Gershom, whose name means "driven out" or "alien". What we also see in this story is a continuation of Moses as *The Deliverer*. He jumps to the rescue of Reuel's daughters just as he had jumped to the rescue of the Hebrew who was being beaten. God chose a man whom He had already predisposed as a rescuer to be His mouthpiece to His people.

The last couple of verses in this passage tell us many things about Moses and God's people.

- Moses can return to Egypt not as a fugitive but as a prophet. The Pharaoh who chased Moses out is dead.
- The Hebrews are still in trouble. The death of the Pharaoh did not improve their situation.
- The Hebrews finally start to pray and beg God for release. They *"cry out"*.
- God remembers His covenant with Abraham, the father of these people. It's time for action.
- God is an active part of this story. It is, in fact, HIS story not Moses'.

This reading ends with an important point. While Moses is spending time in the desert building a family and learning about life in that region, God has *not* forgotten the plight of His people. Even though the Pharaoh who chased Moses from Egypt has died, the new Pharaoh (most likely son to the previous Pharaoh) has the same inclination toward the Hebrews and continues their bitter enslavement.

God saw the people of Israel—and God knew.

So often we believe that God doesn't see our struggle. Or maybe He sees it and doesn't care enough to do something about it. But that is never true. When I give meditation to the past events in my life, I am inundated with times and situations where I struggled to know that God cared about my problem or even actually knew about it. But those are false thoughts. God sees and God knows.

Discussion Questions:

We need to look at the times we stepped in God's way and yet His plan moved forward. How does He get around our "helpful" actions?

When has God clearly seen your struggles and stepped in to help you? What are your prayers in those times? Which gets more of your time and energy: complaining to others or going before the LORD?

In Psalm 142, God is slowly moving Moses through some serious changes. He protected the infant Moses from certain death by giving him a brilliant mother, a faithful sister, and a princess with a compassionate heart. But we also see a Moses who messes up big time – to the point of murder. But God does not abandon Moses or His plan. This psalm was written by David while he hid in the cave from King Saul, who was seeking to end David's life one way or another. The story is recorded for us in 1 Samuel 24. It's worth reading (either again or for the first time) because it shows us what a heart shaped by God can look like when life becomes a struggle.

Watch video #6 "We All Mess Up" that accompanies this lesson at Visual Faith™ Ministry: Movable Adventure Bible Study
visualfaithmin.org/movablebiblestudy

Close with prayer.

the WORD speaks

PSALM 23.
God's Confidence in God, IN.
A Psalm of David
THE LORD is "my shep
shall not want.
2 He maketh me to lie
green pastures: "he lea
side the 'still waters
"He restoreth my
... me in

we ALL mess up!

Study Unit 2 #3

• Carolyn Bira • Dionne Lovstad Jones •
• Jenny Long •

IRREPARABLE?

Dionne — AS a MOM:
• Daughter struggled
• God can repair
• "TAPE TOGETHER" edges (washi)

Jenny — AS a TEACHER:
• So many decisions!
• Parents/Students make bad choices
• No one out of God's Reach
• "HOLY HUDDLE" - people standing w/us
• "Stories to Tell" - how God worked

Carolyn — As a PASTOR'S WIFE:
• People think God can't fix
• Look back - see how God repaired
• Faith stories from others BUILD our faith

What happens when you rely on your own STRENGTH?

need to:
— give up CONTROL
— stop spending your OWN RESOURCES
— REALIGN your day
— Let God TRANSFORM into significance

MOSES kills an EGYPTIAN

• Acted ALONE
• In SECRET
• Relied on OWN STRENGTH
• Became a FUGITIVE

God still works "in spite of"

moves MOSES new location new training

PSALM 90 - only Psalm ascribed to Moses
v. 12 - 17
☑ number our days
☑ satisfy us in the morning
☑ rejoice / be GLAD
☑ establish the work of Your HANDS
our work be GOD'S WORK

my work in GOD'S HANDS

Sketchnote by Karen Bosch @karlyb

My Sketchnotes

Unit Two

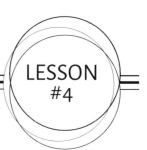

Personal Application Exercise - Lectio Divina

Letting God's Word seep into your spirit, mind, and future behavior.

**Watch video #7 "Lectio Divina" that accompanies this lesson at
Visual Faith™ Ministry: Movable Adventure Bible Study
visualfaithmin.org/movablebiblestudy**

This video shows an example of how to do Lectio Divina in a small group setting.

Psalm 142 *(ESV)*

¹With my voice I cry out to the Lord; with my voice I plead for mercy to the Lord.

²I pour out my complaint before him; I tell my trouble before him.

³When my spirit faints within me, you know my way! In the path where I walk they have hidden a trap for me.

⁴Look to the right and see: there is none who takes notice of me; no refuge remains to me; no one cares for my soul.

⁵I cry to you, O Lord; I say, "You are my refuge, my portion in the land of the living."

⁶Attend to my cry, for I am brought very low! Deliver me from my persecutors, for they are too strong for me!

⁷Bring me out of prison, that I may give thanks to your name! The righteous will surround me, for you will deal bountifully with me.

Step One: You can use "Palms Down-Palms Up", A Breath Prayer, Simple Deep Breathing, or whatever works for you.

After everyone is settled (if you are in a small group), open with prayer.

Selected Text: *Psalm 142:7*

Listening to the Living Word of God – Christ Jesus in the Scriptures:

1. Read the passage aloud **twice,** remaining attentive to some segment that is especially meaningful.

2. SILENCE: 3–5 minutes. Each hears and silently meditates on a word or phrase that stands out.

3. Write down a simple statement containing only a few words, or a theme, that stands out to you. (Share aloud if working with a small group. **No elaboration.**)

How Christ the Word speaks to ME:

1. Second reading of same passage (by another person).

2. SILENCE: 5–7 minutes. Reflect on: Where does the content of this reading touch my life today?

3. Write a brief sentence filling in: "I hear, I see …" (If you are in a small group share your understanding with others.)

What Christ the Word invites me to DO:

1. Third reading (by still another person).

2. SILENCE: 9–11 minutes. Reflect on: I believe that God wants me to … today/this week/this year.

3. Write one or two sentences describing what God is moving you to do based on this text. (If you are in a small group share your response with others.)

Close with prayer.

Favorite Scripture Verse from Unit 2

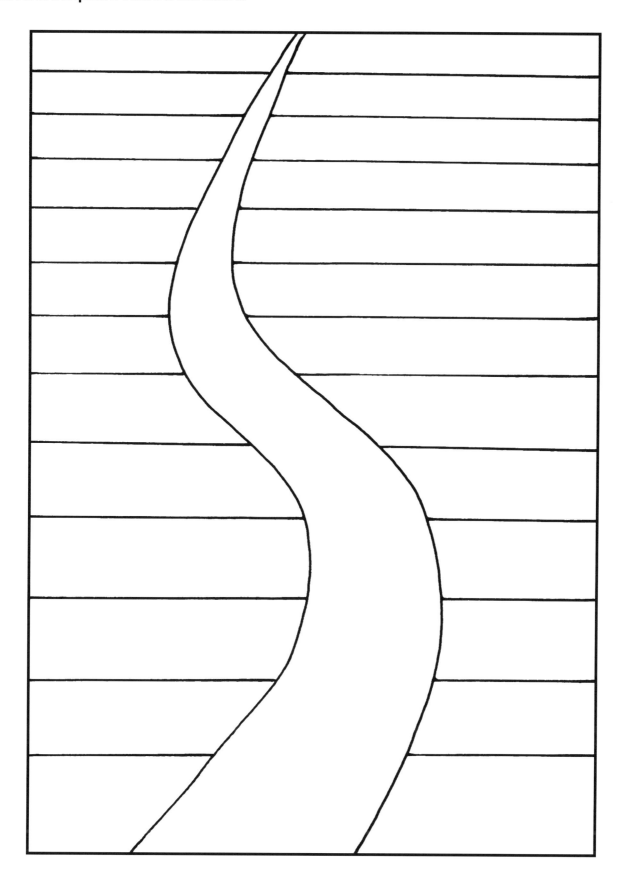

Unit Three

What's in a Name?

Open with prayer.

Gracious Lᴏʀᴅ God (Yahweh Elohim). All praise and honor are due Your magnificent name. Your greatness is declared in all the earth and in the heavens above. May those same praises for You resound in our hearts and minds, as we join with the angels to declare, "Alleluia to the Lord Most High!" Join us here as we engage in Your Word. Fill our minds and spirits with Your truth. Bind us to a certainty about who You are and how You deal so graciously with us. Expand our understanding of You and Your ways, that we might be more solidly attached to You. Transform our thinking, that we might be ever-changed in ways that serve Your Kingdom and declare Your glory. In the name of Jesus, our Savior, we pray. Amen.

Opening Activity

In the box below, take a few minutes and write down all of the Names of God that you know. You can look in your Bible if you want, but get down the ones you already know first. You may work alone or as a group. See how many you can remember. Some have already been supplied for you on the next page. You can also listen to this song for some ideas: You Are Holy (Prince of Peace) by Michael W. Smith. (A link is available at visulfaithmin.org/movablebiblestudy)

אֶהְיֶה אֲשֶׁר אֶהְיֶה

I AM   who   I AM
Yahweh / Jehovah
Adonai

Adonai
Master
Psalm 8:1
"O Lord, our Lord"
Jehovah Adonai

Ezekiel 16:8
"LORD God"
Yahweh Adonai

El Shaddai
All Sufficient
God Almighty
Genesis 17:1–3
"I am God Almighty"

Genesis 35:11
"I am God Almighty"

Elohim
All Powerful
Plural—Trinity
Genesis 1:1–3
Creator God

Deuteronomy 10:17
"LORD your God"
Yahweh Elohim

Immanuel
God with Us
Isaiah 7:14
"... virgin shall bear a Son,
and shall call His name
Immanuel."

Jehovah-Shalom
The LORD is Peace
Numbers 6:22–27
Aaronic Blessing

Isaiah 9:6
"... Everlasting Father,
Prince of Peace."

אֶהְיֶה אֲשֶׁר אֶהְיֶה

I AM   Who   I AM
Yahweh / Jehovah
Self-Existent
Exodus 3:14

Jehovah-Rapha
The LORD Who Heals
Exodus 15:26
"... for I am the LORD your
Healer."
Psalm 103:3; 147:3

Jehovah-Tsidkenu
The LORD our Righteousness
Jeremiah 23:5–6
Jeremiah 33:16
Ezekiel 36:26–27

Jehovah-Jireh
The LORD will Provide
Genesis 22:13–14
The Lord provided a ram for sacrifice

Psalm 23
"You prepare a table before me ..."

Jehovah-Mekaddishkem
The LORD Who Sanctifies
Exodus 31:12–13

Share your "Name Collage" with your group. What do these names for God mean to you? How do these names bring you clarity about God? How do they inform your knowledge of Him? How might you use the different names of God in prayer?

After 40 years as a prince in Egypt and 40 years as a shepherd in the desert, Moses comes to the pivot point of his life. The LORD, **Yahweh**, appears to him and calls him into the role that would fulfill his purpose in life.

Exodus 3:1–14 *(ESV)*

¹Now Moses was keeping the flock of his father-in-law, Jethro, the priest of Midian, and he led his flock to the west side of the wilderness and came to Horeb, the mountain of God. ²And the angel of the Lord appeared to him in a flame of fire out of the midst of a bush. He looked, and behold, the bush was burning, yet it was not consumed. ³And Moses said, "I will turn aside to see this great sight, why the bush is not burned." ⁴When the Lord saw that he turned aside to see, God called to him out of the bush, "Moses, Moses!" And he said, "Here I am." ⁵Then he said, "Do not come near; take your sandals off your feet, for the place on which you are standing is holy ground." ⁶And he said, "I am the God of your father, the God of Abraham, the God of Isaac, and the God of Jacob." And Moses hid his face, for he was afraid to look at God. ⁷Then the Lord said, "I have surely seen the affliction of my people who are in Egypt and have heard their cry because of their taskmasters. I know their sufferings, ⁸and I have come down to deliver them out of the hand of the Egyptians and to bring them up out of that land to a good and broad land, a land flowing with milk and honey, to the place of the Canaanites, the Hittites, the Amorites, the Perizzites, the Hivites, and the Jebusites. ⁹And now, behold, the cry of the people of Israel has come to me, and I have also seen the oppression with which the Egyptians oppress them. ¹⁰Come, I will send you to Pharaoh that you may bring my people, the children of Israel, out of Egypt." ¹¹But Moses said to God, "Who am I that I should go to Pharaoh and bring the children of Israel out of Egypt?" ¹²He said, "But I will be with you, and this shall be the sign for you, that I have sent you: when you have brought the people out of Egypt, you shall serve God on this mountain." ¹³Then Moses said to God, "If I come to the people of Israel and say to them, 'The God of your fathers has sent me to you,' and they ask me, 'What is his name?' what shall I say to them?" ¹⁴God said to Moses, "I Am who I Am." And he said, "Say this to the people of Israel, 'I Am has sent me to you.'"

Moses has wandered far from his home in Midian in search of good grazing land for his sheep. He finds himself at Mt. Horeb (also believed by many to be Mt. Sinai; the same Mt. Sinai where several months later Moses will meet with God and receive the 10 Commandments). A most unusual sight awaits him; a bush that is burning but not being consumed, just as a candle wick burns but is not consumed with the wax providing the fuel. In this case, God Himself keeps the fire blazing without consuming the actual plant. This is, of course, an incredibly curious thing that Moses simply must investigate.

Exodus 3:14

Watch video #8 "What's in a Name?" that accompanies this lesson at Visual Faith™ Ministry: Movable Adventure Bible Study visualfaithmin.org/movablebiblestudy

Close with prayer.

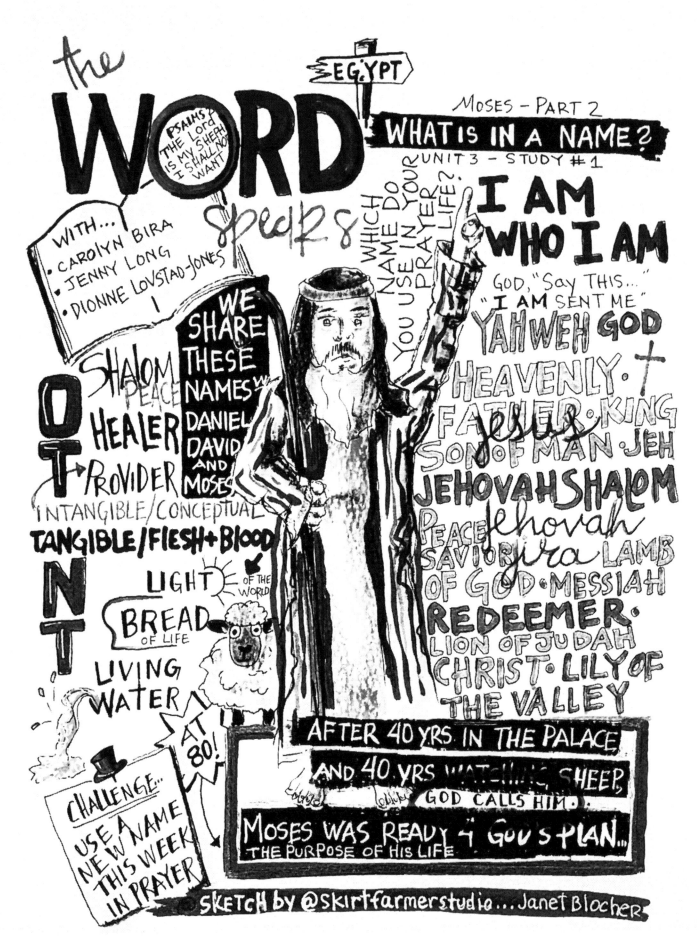

the WORD speaks

PSALMS
THE LORD IS MY SHEPH
IS MY SHEP
I SHALL NO WANT

EGYPT

MOSES – PART 2
WHAT IS IN A NAME?
UNIT 3 – STUDY #1

WITH...
• CAROLYN BIRA
• JENNY LONG
• DIONNE LOVSTAD-JONES
I

WHICH NAME DO YOU USE IN YOUR PRAYER LIFE?

I AM WHO I AM

GOD, "Say This..."
"I AM SENT ME"

YAHWEH GOD
HEAVENLY
FATHER • KING
Jesus
SON OF MAN • JEH
JEHOVAHSHALOM
PEACE Jehovah
SAVIOR Jira LAMB
OF GOD • MESSIAH
REDEEMER •
LION OF JUDAH
CHRIST • LILY OF
THE VALLEY

SHALOM PEACE
OT
HEALER
PROVIDER
INTANGIBLE/CONCEPTUAL
TANGIBLE/FLESH + BLOOD
NT

WE SHARE THESE NAMES w/ DANIEL DAVID AND MOSES

LIGHT
OF THE WORLD
BREAD OF LIFE
LIVING WATER
AT 80!

CHALLENGE...
USE A NEW NAME THIS WEEK IN PRAYER

AFTER 40 YRS IN THE PALACE, AND 40 YRS WATCHING SHEEP, GOD CALLS HIM•

MOSES WAS READY 4 GOD'S PLAN...
THE PURPOSE OF HIS LIFE

SKETCH BY @skirtfarmerstudio...Janet Blocher

My Sketchnotes

Unit Three

The Fire of God

Open with prayer.

Dear Lord God, we come together in Your name to study Your Word. We invite You to engage our hearts, minds, and spirits as You move us deeper into Your love and grace for our lives. Help us to look at the life of your servant, Moses, and find our own walk with You along the way. Give us patience with ourselves and each other as You use Your Word to further shape and form us, that we might love You more and serve You better. In the name of Jesus we pray. Amen.

Opening Activity

In this lesson, we will examine Moses' introduction to God as he acts as shepherd to his father-in-law's sheep. The life of a shepherd was a solitary one. Moses had time to think. Have you ever spent significant time alone? If so, what was that experience like for you? Was it on purpose, such as a spiritual retreat or camping trip, or was it imposed upon you by illness, our national quarantine, or some other kind of circumstance? What did you learn in the silence/solitude?

Some story details:

Moses is wandering near Mt. Sinai. (He's a loooong way from Midian). He is serving as a shepherd for his father-in-law, Jethro. Being a shepherd was considered one of the lowliest of jobs, and one that was loathed by the Egyptians. At this point, Moses is 80 years old and identifying with his own people. If he were to return to Egypt it would be as a Hebrew not an Egyptian Prince. He has little or no personal wealth as an employee (and son-in-law) to Jethro.

A Theophany of Fire

The term "theophany" ("appearance of God") is normally used to refer to instances recorded in Scripture where God appears in some way to humans. God's appearances do not represent his totality or the fullness of his essence. They instead are occasions in which he is visible *in some fashion*—normally, through a shape that is not exactly natural (i.e., he does not look like a human); but he can nevertheless be looked at and focused on by a human, an appearance often accompanied by fire.

Stuart, D. K. ©2006. *Exodus* (Vol. 2, p. 113). Nashville: Broadman & Holman Publishers.

The burning bush is not the first or only time God chooses to appear with fire. In fact, the instances are numerous. A way to access all of these passages quickly is to assign one or two of the references to a person or group of people. They look up their assignment and report back to the large group. Even though the following list is lengthy, and you may not want to look up all of the references, at least look up some of them. There is some sense of power and awe in God's use of fire. Looking up and reading through these passages can only enhance your appreciation of this aspect of God.

Appearance to ...	Fire / Object	Bible Reference
Abraham and the Covenant	A firepot and a torch	Genesis 15:17
The Children of Israel in the Wilderness	A Pillar of Fire by Night A Pillar of Cloud by Day	Exodus 13:21
Moses and the 10 Commandments	Fire on Mt. Sinai	Exodus 19:18
Elijah defeats the Baal worshipers	Fire from God consumes the Altar	1 Kings 18:20-40
God Identified as or accompanied by fire		Deuteronomy 4:24, 36 Psalm 50:3
Isaiah	God's wrath and rebuke comes with fire / on His fiery chariot	Isaiah 66:15
Daniel's Vision	A throne of fire	Daniel 7:9
Apostle John	Jesus has Eyes of Fire	Revelation 1:14; 2:18; 19:12
God's Judgment	Destructive Power	Numbers 11:1-3; 16:35; 2 Kings 1:12-14 Job 1:16 Amos 1:4-2:5
Pentecost	The Holy Spirit Descends as Tongues of Fire	Acts 2:1-13

Discussion Questions:

Even though we think of fire as destructive, it is also extremely useful. Why do you think God chooses to use this destructive, beautiful, powerful, useful, terrifying element? What does that concept bring to your understanding of who God is?

Exodus 3:1–14 (ESV)

¹Now Moses was keeping the flock of his father-in-law, Jethro, the priest of Midian, and he led his flock to the west side of the wilderness and came to Horeb, the mountain of God. ²And the angel of the Lord appeared to him in a flame of fire out of the midst of a bush. He looked, and behold, the bush was burning, yet it was not consumed. ³And Moses said, "I will turn aside to see this great sight, why the bush is not burned." ⁴When the Lord saw that he turned aside to see, God called to him out of the bush, "Moses, Moses!" And he said, "Here I am." ⁵Then he said, "Do not come near; take your sandals off your feet, for the place on which you are standing is holy ground." ⁶And he said, "I am the God of your father, the God of Abraham, the God of Isaac, and the God of Jacob." And Moses hid his face, for he was afraid to look at God. ⁷Then the Lord said, "I have surely seen the affliction of my people who are in Egypt and have heard their cry because of their taskmasters. I know their sufferings, ⁸and I have come down to deliver them out of the hand of the Egyptians and to bring them up out of that land to a good and broad land, a land flowing with milk and honey, to the place of the Canaanites, the Hittites, the Amorites, the Perizzites, the Hivites, and the Jebusites. ⁹And now, behold, the cry of the people of Israel has come to me, and I have also seen the oppression with which the Egyptians oppress them. ¹⁰Come, I will send you to Pharaoh that you may bring my people, the children of

Israel, out of Egypt." [11] But Moses said to God, "Who am I that I should go to Pharaoh and bring the children of Israel out of Egypt?" [12] He said, "But I will be with you, and this shall be the sign for you, that I have sent you: when you have brought the people out of Egypt, you shall serve God on this mountain." [13] Then Moses said to God, "If I come to the people of Israel and say to them, 'The God of your fathers has sent me to you,' and they ask me, 'What is his name?' what shall I say to them?" [14] God said to Moses, "I Am who I Am." And he said, "Say this to the people of Israel, 'I Am has sent me to you.'"

An interesting detail:

As Moses becomes engaged in this conversation with God [a burning bush!], a couple of things happen. With the speaking of the words, "Moses, Moses!" God begins a conversation with a man who probably knows very little about Him. God's first words indicate to Moses a sense of care, concern, and intimacy. Whenever a person's name was spoken twice it was an indication of good will and friendship. The Bible has a few more examples of God using this term of endearment when calling upon His people. Look up each of these passages and read some of the surrounding text. What are the circumstances involved in these events?

- Matthew 23:37 ("Jerusalem, Jerusalem")

- 1 Samuel 3:10 ("Samuel, Samuel")

- Matthew 27:46 ("Eli, Eli")

- Acts 9:4 ("Saul, Saul")

Imagine God calling your name. Doodle/write/decorate your name TWICE in the space below. As you do that, take a few moments, and just listen. That's hard. But it's worth it. The listening part may also be something that you're going to have learn to do. We're not really taught how to listen to God.

What would He say to you? How would it feel to be addressed by the God of the Universe as He uses a form of endearment?

Close with prayer.

Unit Three

Take off Your Shoes

Mother Teresa was once asked during an interview with Dan Rather what she said to God when she prayed. "I don't say much," replied Mother Teresa, "mostly I just listen." "And what does God say to you?" asked the interviewer. "He doesn't say much," she replied. "Mostly He just listens. And if you don't understand that, I can't explain it to you."

Opening Question:

This is rather a remarkable story and contains some interesting insight in the prayer life of someone who walked on the front lines of Christianity for a long time, garnering great respect along the way. Clearly, she had a close, personal relationship with Jesus. She heard Him call her name. What would you say about your prayer life, if asked? Share your answer with the group.

Open with prayer.

Lord God, we praise You and thank You for this chance to be in Your Word. Please join us here through the power of Your Holy Spirit and fill this time with Your wisdom, grace, and love for us. Help us come to a deeper understanding of Your desire to spend time with us. Inspire in our lives that same desire when it comes to giving You this most precious commodity of time. Ignite in us a love for You that turns our attention toward You with great expectation. In Jesus' name we pray. Amen.

Our story continues:

Of course Moses' curiosity is piqued, and he steps closer to learn more. God then sets the parameters for the conversation, helping Moses understand what it means to stand in His presence. Moses now stands on holy ground; it's time to stay back at a respectful distance and remove his sandals as a sign that he recognizes God's holiness (and perhaps his own unworthiness). Joshua, Moses' right-hand man and the one who takes over leadership of Israel when Moses dies, also has a similar circumstance as he prepares to enter the Promised Land with God's people.

Joshua 5:13–15 (ESV)

[13]When Joshua was by Jericho, he lifted up his eyes and looked, and behold, a man was standing before him with his drawn sword in his hand. And Joshua went to him and said to him, "Are you for us, or for our adversaries?" [14]And he said, "No; but I am the commander of the army of the LORD. Now I have come." And Joshua fell on his face to the earth and worshiped and said to him, "What does my lord say to his servant?" [15]And the commander of the LORD's army said to Joshua, "Take off your sandals from your feet, for the place where you are standing is holy." And Joshua did so.

These two instances (Exodus 3:5 and Joshua 5:15) are the only time in all of the Bible when someone is told to remove their shoes in the presence of God. In that regard, they are unique. God calls the ground upon which He and Moses are having this conversation *holy*. What makes it holy is the presence of God. We might call other ground holy, but God does not.

Discussion Questions:

God uses something weird (a burning, unconsumed bush) to get Moses' attention. God uses all kinds of things to draw us closer. What does God use to draw you to Himself? What makes you move toward Him and His voice? In what ways does your relationship with God grow, change, or deepen in those times?

But God, I Can't

- **We all try to tell God, "no, I don't want to". Moses expresses his reluctance with, "Who am I …"**

   ¹¹But Moses said to God, "Who am I that I should go to Pharaoh and bring the children of Israel out of Egypt?"

- **But God has chosen Moses and promises to equip him.**

   ¹²"But I will be with you, and this shall be the sign for you, that I have sent you: when you have brought the people out of Egypt, you shall serve God on this mountain."

- **God promises help, guidance, and eventually, he will have his brother Aaron to help as well.**

God gives a sign to Moses in the moment by changing Moses' staff into a snake and making his hand leprous. (To read this story in detail, look at Exodus 4:1–17. There you will find the story of these two signs and God assigning Aaron to be Moses' helper.)

Moses explains to God that he is unable to lead the people. God lets him know it won't be a problem. Looking back on your life, has God ever equipped you to do something you believed you couldn't do? What was the outcome? What did you learn about yourself? About God?

Moses' life in Egypt taught him that there are many gods (polytheism) and that mixing religious beliefs (syncretism) is normal. And so he asks God, "which one are you?" Neither of these beliefs are acceptable to God. By introducing Himself as I AM who I Am, YAHWEH is claiming ONLYNESS. Moses knows that is going to be a problem for the Egyptian Pharaoh. (God makes short business of the Egyptian belief in numerous gods of nature through the Ten Plagues – but that's another study.) Next, we will dive into the name that God uses to introduce Himself to Moses.

Watch video #9 "Take Off Your Shoes" that accompanies this lesson at Visual Faith™ Ministry: Movable Adventure Bible Study visualfaithmin.org/movablebiblestudy

To close out this lesson, spend some time taking those things you believe are too much for God to ask of you before Him in prayer. Perhaps share some of those events, situations, or circumstances with your group.

Close with prayer.

The WORD speaks

PSALMS 23
THE LORD IS
MY SHEPHERD
I SHALL NOT
WANT. HE
MAKETH ME

TAKE OFF YOUR SHOES...

with:
CAROLYN BIRA
DIONNE LOVSTAD-JONES
JENNY LONG

WHAT SHOES IS THE LORD PREPARING YOU 2 FILL?

HELLO I AM WHO I AM
GOD OF YOUR FATHER AND THE GOD OF ABRAHAM, ISAAC AND JACOB

MOSES PART 2 UNIT 3 #3

YOU ARE STANDING ON HOLY GROUND

THE PALACE SLIPPER & THE SHEPHERD'S SANDAL CAME BEFORE THE BARE FEET OF

PRAYER SHHHH

IS A CONVERSATION ①

② A GIVE AND TAKE

TIME WITH YOUR
③ HEAVENLY FATHER
NOT A "GIVE ME" SESSION
ON SANTA'S LAP

TO DO

⑤

MY BURNING BUSH STORY...
SERVITUDE
JOB
• ADOPTION
DM •

④ TAKE TIME 2 PRAISE

WRITE THEM DOWN

HOW DID JESUS SHOW UP IN YOUR DAY?

DAY

SKETCHED BY: @SKIRTfarmerstudio   JANET BLOCHER

My Sketchnotes

Unit Three

The Great I Am

Open with prayer.

Spend a few moments in silence, with each person listing those things that serve as distractions when it comes to a vibrant prayer life. What claims your attention when you are trying to give it to God?

Opening Activity

Share your list of distractions with the group. Brainstorm ways you can be more focused during your intentional prayer time each day. What are some new strategies you can try?

אֶהְיֶה אֲשֶׁר אֶהְיֶה **Learning God's Name**

The first exercise in the study invited you to think about the myriad of names God provides us for Himself. While reading the Old Testament, we find that the writers almost always tell us what someone's name means. In our culture, we give a child a name for all kinds of reasons, but generally we don't pay that much attention to what a name means. In some segments of our culture, names are contrived to give a baby something unique or something that is a combination of family names. God's name is magnificent, in that He bears several names that describe in detail who He is and what He does. When God introduces Himself to Moses, it is the culmination of 80 years of life where God has carefully exposed Moses to all that he will need in order to further God's plan. Now, Moses is instructed on how to proceed. God's name plays a huge part in that plan.

Exodus 3:13–22 (ESV)

¹³Then Moses said to God, "If I come to the people of Israel and say to them, 'The God of your fathers has sent me to you,' and they ask me, 'What is his name?' what shall I say to them?" ¹⁴God said to Moses, "I AM who I AM." And he said, "Say this to the people of Israel, 'I AM has sent me to you.'"

¹⁵God also said to Moses, "Say this to the people of Israel, 'The Lord, the God of your fathers, the God of Abraham, the God of Isaac, and the God of Jacob, has sent me to you.' This is my name forever, and thus I am to be remembered throughout all generations. ¹⁶Go and gather the elders of Israel together and say to them, 'The Lord, the God of your fathers, the God of Abraham, of Isaac, and of Jacob, has appeared to me, saying, "I have observed you and what has been done to you in Egypt, ¹⁷and I promise that I will bring you up out of the affliction of Egypt to the land of the Canaanites, the Hittites, the Amorites, the Perizzites, the Hivites, and the Jebusites, a land flowing with milk and honey."' ¹⁸And they will listen to your voice, and you and the elders of Israel shall go to the king of Egypt and say to him, 'The Lord, the God of the Hebrews, has met with us; and now, please let us go a three days' journey into the wilderness, that we may sacrifice to the Lord our God.' ¹⁹But I know that the king of Egypt will not let you go unless compelled by a mighty hand. ²⁰So I will stretch out my hand and strike Egypt with all the wonders that I will do in it; after that he will let you go. ²¹And I will give this people favor in the sight of the Egyptians; and when you go, you shall not go empty, ²²but each woman shall ask of her neighbor, and any woman who lives in her house, for silver and gold jewelry, and for clothing. You shall put them on your sons and on your daughters. So you shall plunder the Egyptians."

Discussion Questions:

As we are well into our study of the impact, importance, and power of God's name, consider how we minimize His majesty and sovereignty over us. Our culture has minimized and denigrated God's name through flippant usage as an expression of surprise, shock, or even just minor annoyance. Do the words "Oh my God" ever pass over your lips? Have you every typed OMG into an email or text? Or do you cringe every time someone uses this phrase around you? What impact does that common usage of God's name have on you?

Yahweh = "I Am who I Am"

These words mean "I Exist". In that moment Moses knows that this is the Creator God who has always been. "I Exist" points to the fact that God is eternal; He has always been and will always be. Moses knows, despite living in a polytheistic world, he is meeting the only One True God. This isn't the first time the name *Yahweh* is heard or used in reference to God. The first time is in Genesis 1:3. "God said, 'Let there be light'." He uses His own name to call all things into existence. "Let there be light" is "Yahweh light" in Hebrew. We also find Yahweh as the name God used in the stories of Noah, Abraham, Isaac, and Jacob. All of them knew this name but they generally refer to Him as God Almighty. God's name had probably fallen away during the time the Children of Israel spend as slaves in Egypt (400 years). The Hebrews may have lost their knowledge of the true God! And so, God reintroduces Himself to Moses, and thus to Israel.

This is the same God that we worship today – the Eternal I AM. Just to be allowed to speak the name of God is a privilege and an honor. This is the God who created all things, called Abraham out of the darkness of paganism, anointed David as King, and sent Jesus into the world to die for our sins. We do a disservice to God and even to ourselves to take that name lightly or misuse it in any way. Jesus lays claim to the title of "I AM" and we bow down to Him with humble gratitude that the Great I AM shed His blood for our sin. Like Moses, we stand in humble awe and adoration.

Extra Information

This study leans rather heavily upon the name "Yahweh". That is what the Lᴏʀᴅ uses to introduce Himself to Moses. But, we also need to address the name "Jehovah", which we hear with frequency today. This grew out of the Jewish tradition of not being allowed to even utter the name of God with human tongues.

Jehovah

Strictly speaking, this is the only name of God in the Bible. The other terms point to aspects of His character or of His relations with people *Jehovah* is actually a word that was created in the Middle Ages by the rabbis. Reverent Jews traditionally did not pronounce the proper name of God when they encountered it in the Hebrew text. That word was apparently to be pronounced as *Yahweh*. Instead they substituted the word *Adonai*, "Master," "Lord." Several centuries after Christ Jewish scholars inserted the vowels of Adonai between the semivowels and consonants (. and h) of *Yahweh*, thus creating *Jehovah*.

Although the term Jehovah is found before Ex. 3, in that chapter God speaks of Himself as the self-existent One who is able to keep promises all by Himself. Many scholars make a connection between the name and the phrase *I am* from the verb *to be*. If this association is correct *Yahweh, Jehovah* has to do with independent existence. It would thus point to the God of the Bible as the only entity in the universe that does not depend on anything else. This is, of course, a perfectly appropriate name for Him, since He is the Creator of all things, and everything depends on Him. *Yahweh/Jehovah* teaches us through His personal name that He is unique, powerful, different from every other being, the sustainer of everything, and the One who alone can keep His promises perfectly. It is the name especially of the covenant-keeping God of Israel.

Karleen, P. S. ©1987. *The Handbook to Bible Study* (p. 203). New York: Oxford University Press.

**Watch video #10 "The Great I Am" that accompanies this lesson at
Visual Faith™ Ministry: Movable Adventure Bible Study
visualfaithmin.org/movablebiblestudy**

Close with prayer.

the WORD speaks

PSALMS 23 THE LORD IS MY SHEPHERD I SHALL NOT WANT. HE MAKE

THE GREAT I AM

SON of MAN + SON of GOD

YAHWEH

(I EXIST)

CAROLYN BIRA
DIONNE LOUSTAD-JONES
JENNY&LONG

THE VINE
LIVING WATER
BREAD OF LIFE
THE GOOD SHEPHERD

HIS NAMES REVEAL HIMSELF TO US

ALL CREATION WILL SEE THE DIETY OF JESUS CHRIST

"OH MY GOD"
"OMG..."
IS A MISUSE of GOD'S NAME
INSTEAD

LIFT UP THE NAME OF JESUS

HE WAS HUMILIATED AND EXALTED IN THE SAME PASSAGE

WE NEED 2 RECOGNIZE THE POWER IN HIS NAME

AT THE NAME OF JESUS, EVERY KNEE SHALL BOW, AND EVERY TONGUE CONFESS THAT JESUS CHRIST IS LORD.
-PHILIPPIANS 2:5-11

SKETCHED BY JANET BLOCHER @skirtfarmerstudio

My Sketchnotes

Unit Three

ἐγώ εἰμί

> **Greek: I AM → ἐγώ εἰμί**
> ἐγώ egō; I (only expressed when emphatic) —**myself**
> εἰμί eimi; *I exist, I am*

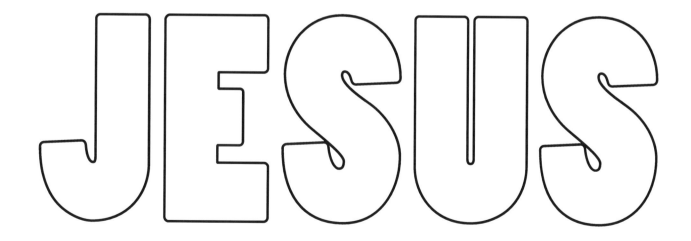

Open with prayer.

Dear Lord Jesus, Redeemer and Friend. We are joyful to be able to speak with You openly and freely. That the God of the Universe would grant such a privilege to His creation is amazing. We bask in your great love and give You praise for such a gift. Jesus, would You please join us here today as we continue in Your Word. Show us what it means that You appropriated the name of Yahweh. Fill us with awe and wonder as we remember that You are indeed God. In Your dear name we pray. Amen.

Opening Activity

Using the name of Jesus written below, write the name of those you want to see draw closer to the Lord. Who do you pray for, that they may come to faith, or know the Lord better? Put them in the letters below. Pray for them as you are adding their names.

Jesus – the Great I AM

In Exodus 3, God tells Moses His name. This is a huge moment and one that Jesus Himself accesses as He speaks with His disciples, the eavesdropping crowd, and the Pharisees. The Son of God declares Himself to be "*I AM*".

John 14:6 *(ESV)*

*Jesus said to him, "**I AM** the way, and the truth, and the life. No one comes to the Father except through me.*

The Bible, while made up of 66 books, is one long story. It is the story of God's plan for His people. So for His Son, Jesus, to refer to the beginning of the story comes as no surprise. But it is a beautiful connection to the truth of Jesus' deity. When we read the words, "*I AM the way, the truth, and the life ...*" we must hear the name of Yahweh resound through our hearts and minds. Jesus and Yahweh are one and the same.

There are several instances in the Gospels of Jesus claiming the name of God as His own. Those conversations bring struggle for Jesus' enemies and awe to the hearts of believers. In the Greek, the language of the New Testament, I AM is expressed by the words Ego Eimi (pronounced EGGO' A'MY).

Jesus employs the verse from Exodus 3:14 as He is in a heated and rather ugly debate with the Pharisees. They have called Him satanic. They have lobbed every insult they can imagine right in His face. If you want a feeling for the whole story, read all of John 8. This chapter contains it all: Jesus, the Compassionate Forgiver as He deals with the woman caught in adultery, Jesus the great "I AM" teaching the Pharisees that He is indeed Lord (Yahweh) over all things.

Discussion Questions:

Why is it important that Jesus associates Himself so closely with Yahweh? So closely that He uses God's own name as shared with Moses?

John 8:48–59 *(ESV)*

⁴⁸*The Jews answered him, "Are we not right in saying that you are a Samaritan and have a demon?"* ⁴⁹*Jesus answered,* "I do not have a demon, but I honor my Father, and you dishonor me. ⁵⁰Yet I do not seek my own glory; there is One who seeks it, and he is the judge. ⁵¹Truly, truly, I say to you, if anyone keeps my word, he will never see death." ⁵²*The Jews said to him, "Now we know that you have a demon! Abraham died, as did the prophets, yet you say, 'If anyone keeps my word, he will never taste death.'* ⁵³*Are you greater than our father Abraham, who died? And the prophets died! Who do you make yourself out to be?"* ⁵⁴*Jesus answered,* "If I glorify myself, my glory is nothing. It is my Father who glorifies me, of whom you say, 'He is our God.' ⁵⁵But you have not known him. I know him. If I were to say that I do not know him, I would be a liar like you, but I do know him and I keep his word. ⁵⁶Your father Abraham rejoiced that he would see my day. He saw it and was glad." ⁵⁷*So the Jews said to him, "You are not yet fifty years old, and have you seen Abraham?"* ⁵⁸*Jesus said to them,* "Truly, truly, I say to you, before Abraham was, **I AM**." ⁵⁹*So they picked up stones to throw at him, but Jesus hid himself and went out of the temple.*

In these instances (and several others) the Greek text says "I am". That's all. Translators have added "I am *he*", or "I am *here*". But what we find in this conversation is Jesus undeniably declaring that He and the Father are One – The Lᴏʀᴅ. With that title, Jesus is pointing to the time when Moses is introduced to The Lᴏʀᴅ in the burning bush. He is telling the Pharisees, "I AM was there. I AM is here! And you don't know Him".

Now read John 18:1–9. This event takes place in the Garden of Gethsemane. These are the moments when Judas' plan of betrayal plays out in all of its ugliness. Judas brings the guards who work for the Pharisees right to Jesus. To be arrested.

John 18:1–9 *(ESV)*

¹*When he had finished praying, Jesus left with his disciples and crossed the Kidron Valley. On the other side there was a garden, and he and his disciples went into it.* ²*Now Judas, who betrayed him, knew the place, because Jesus had often met there with his disciples.* ³*So Judas came to the garden, guiding a detachment of soldiers and some officials from the chief priests and the Pharisees. They were carrying torches, lanterns and weapons.* ⁴*Jesus, knowing all that was going to happen to him, went out and asked them,* "Who is it you want?" ⁵*"Jesus of Nazareth," they replied.* "**I AM** (he)," *Jesus said. (And Judas the traitor was standing there with them.)* ⁶*When Jesus said,* "**I AM** (he)," ***they drew back and fell to the ground***. ⁷*Again he asked them,* "Who is it you want?" *"Jesus of Nazareth," they said.* ⁸*Jesus answered,* "I told you that I **AM** (he). If you are looking for me, then let these men go." ⁹*This happened so that the words he had spoken would be fulfilled: "I have not lost one of those you gave me."*

We simply must take a moment here and visualize that scene. Jesus has poured out his anguish over upcoming events to His Father. Now He patiently and quietly faces the man who has betrayed his location to the Pharisees. They've sent a detachment of soldiers to arrest Jesus. When asked if He is Jesus of Nazareth, He merely answers with "I AM". *And they fall to the ground!!!!* No one can stand in the presence of Almighty God, the Great I AM. His authority cannot be denied.

Discussion Question:

Visualize a detachment of soldiers falling down before the Lᴏʀᴅ of All. Where does that incident take your heart and mind?

_____

_____

_____

_____

_____

_____

_____

Finally, we examine Paul's words to the Church in Philippi. This passage seems to logically follows this amazing incident.

Philippians 2:5–11 *(ESV)*

⁵Have this mind among yourselves, which is yours in Christ Jesus, ⁶who, though he was in the form of God, did not count equality with God a thing to be grasped, ⁷but emptied himself, by taking the form of a servant, being born in the likeness of men. ⁸And being found in human form, he humbled himself by becoming obedient to the point of death, even death on a cross. ⁹Therefore God has highly exalted him and bestowed on him the name that is above every name, ¹⁰so that at the name of Jesus every knee should bow, in heaven and on earth and under the earth, ¹¹and every tongue confess that Jesus Christ is Lord, to the glory of God the Father.

Perhaps those soldiers and the disciples saw but a glimpse of what is to come when Yahweh returns for His Bride, the Church. How does this passage illuminate our stance before I AM?

_____

_____

_____

_____

_____

Below, you will find the words I AM. Inside of those letters, or around the outside, write or illustrate your response to the Great I AM. Reflect on what it means to fall down before the Great I AM. You could write out a prayer of praise, draw people around the name of God that you want to bring into His throne room today, or just color them in as you ponder the greatness of God. Let your imagination and the Spirit take you wherever He wants you to go. Share what you've written, drawn, or thought about with your group if you are doing this study with others.

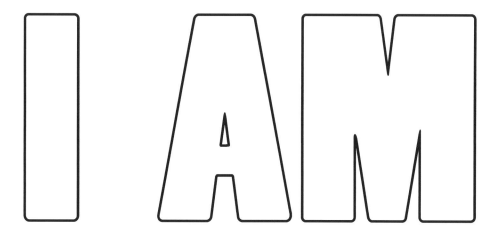

Close with prayer.

Unit Three

God Knows

Open with prayer.

Spend 5 minutes, using the graph paper below, to write out a *secret code prayer*.

Watch video #11 "Secret Code Prayer" by Valerie Matyas that accompanies this lesson at Visual Faith™ Ministry: Movable Adventure Bible Study
visualfaithmin.org/movablebiblestudy
You can learn exactly how to do the "Secret Code Prayer" in this 5 minute video.

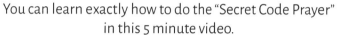

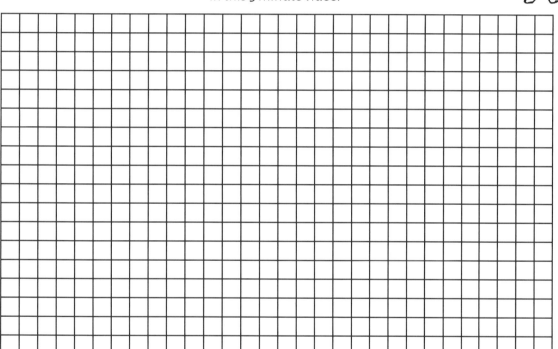

God Involves Moses in His Plan

God gives Moses a rare and detailed look at what is coming in the future. That would be a rare occurrence for most of us! God does not share what is coming up even though that might be extremely convenient. But, for most of us, that would be a terrible thing to know. We would mess that up in no time. A favorite Bible passage for many is Psalm 119:105. *Thy Word is a Lamp unto my feet and a Light unto my path.* These words bring to mind the image of walking through the forest at night. Your lantern or flashlight only shows you where to put the next step. God is trustworthy enough to lead us when we don't know what's coming or what to do next. All we need to know is where to place the next footstep.

But in this story from Exodus 3, God deems it important to tell Moses what is coming for him, the Children of Israel, and the Egyptians. And I believe God shares this information for an important reason. It is time for Moses to recognize the sovereignty and power of God. There's work to be done, Moses needs to trust that God is in control in order to move forward. Remember, Moses really doesn't have a great deal of experience with God. He is just getting to know about God and the word relationship can't really be used yet. This knowledge of God is in its infancy. But God is asking Moses to trust Him for some really major things What God is promising Moses is monumental not only for Moses but for an entire nation. God promises Moses several things:

- **God Himself is in control**
- **He's the God of their forefathers**
- **God sees His people mistreated and in slavery, and He doesn't like it**
- **God promises to bring His people out of Egypt and free them from bondage**
- **God promises to lead them into the Promised Land**
- **God promises Moses the people *will* listen to him**
- **God informs Moses that the Pharaoh will not cooperate**
- **God promises to "compel" the Pharaoh**
- **God promises the Egyptians will be plundered by His people**

All of these promises pile up before Moses. He is challenged to believe that God does indeed have the power to do as He says He will. God has made promises to us as well. We have the same opportunity to trust that God will deliver us from our bondage to sin, death, and the power of the devil. We have the benefit of standing on this side of the death and resurrection of Jesus. Promises kept. Now we await the culmination of the final promise—the return of Jesus. He's been a promise keeper so far. There's no reason to doubt He won't keep this last one as well.

Application Concepts

God shares His great concern for the Children of Israel who are still back in Egypt and His plan for Moses to go and speak with the Pharaoh on His behalf. Of course Moses says, "who am I to receive such an assignment." God defines Himself and He is spectacular!

 **Exodus 3:6** *(ESV)*

"I am the God of your father, [Amram] I am the God of Abraham, I am the God of Isaac, I am the God of Jacob"

— **this is all said *in the present tense* because they all still exist *in God's presence!!!***

Exodus 3:7–8 *(ESV)*

[7]Then the Lord said, "I have surely seen the affliction of my people who are in Egypt and have heard their cry because of their taskmasters. I know their sufferings, [8]and I have come down to deliver them out of the hand of the Egyptians and to bring them up out of that land to a good and broad land, a land flowing with milk and honey, to the place of the Canaanites, the Hittites, the Amorites, the Perizzites, the Hivites, and the Jebusites.

God Remembers
(Exodus 2:23–25)
What are the promises of God that you have learned in the past? How do they apply to You today?

God Sees What's Happening
If we believe in a Sovereign God, then we know that He sees all; everything that happens to You. Do you live in that reality? How does it impact your life?

God Hears Your Cries
Sometimes it seems as though our prayers fall to the ground unheard. But that is never true. What things remain on your "prayer list" that you want God to hear?

God Has a Plan for You
What parts of God's plan do you know for sure? How surrendered are you to His plan?

Moses Faces 2 Challenges—As Do We
Trusting God — Moses is just getting to know God. Trusting Him in this major, life-changing endeavor seems risky and Moses is basically unwilling. How do you respond to those types of situations?
(See Job 38–41 for God's response to our doubts)

How can God call a fallible, vulnerable, weak human to carry out His will?
(See Judges 6:11–40 for a similar story.)

Discussion Questions:
When struggles come into your life, rehearsing that God remembers you, see you, hears you, and has a plan can be helpful. What can (or do) you do to bring those truths to mind? What would help you (or helps you) lean into God?

Watch video #12 "God Knows" that accompanies this lesson at
Visual Faith™ Ministry: Movable Adventure Bible Study
visualfaithmin.org/movablebiblestudy

Write out a prayer that invites God into your unsure places. Where does your trust level need to rise in order for you to move forward? Seek His face for a deeper trust. Hold up those times where He faithfully brought you through a struggle. Where your footsteps were secure. And don't forget to hold up those times when things didn't turn out the way you would have hoped. It's important that we share *everything* with our Father.

My Sketchnotes

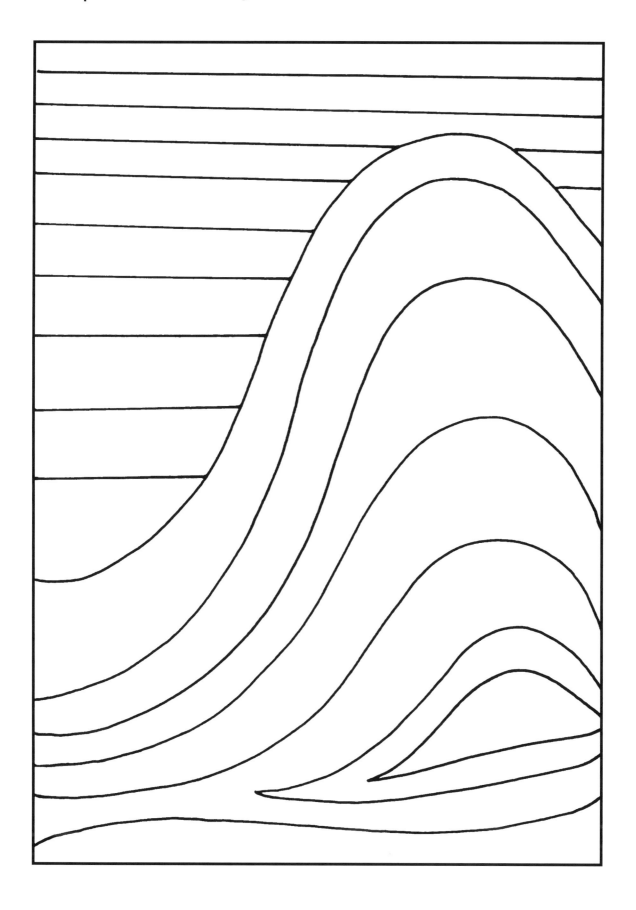

Unit Four

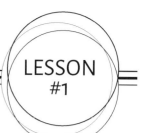

Waiting on God

Open with prayer.

Gracious Lord God, Father, Son, and Holy Spirit. Thank You for this time in Your Word. Holy Spirit, speak so I can understand. Open my mind and heart to Your Word. Help me to be open to Your instruction, insight, inspiration, and challenges. Keep me from distractions or tangents that would draw me away from the changes You are making in me. May You be glorified in this time we are together. May Your presence be palpable. In the name of Jesus I pray. Amen.

Discussion Question:

Have you ever done something so incredibly foolish you can still look back and shudder over how detrimental that was to you or someone else? Today, we are going to examine a story about two old guys and a huge lie. Before we begin, it might be helpful to realize that we've all been there. This isn't going to be a time of "True Confessions". There's no need for that. But it might be helpful to remember how you felt during that time and how you feel about it when you remember it today. Take a few moments and fill in the circle below with some representation of that life event; then surround that circle with words. The words above the circle are how you felt when you participated in whatever activity comes to mind. The words below the circle are how you feel today when you remember that time.

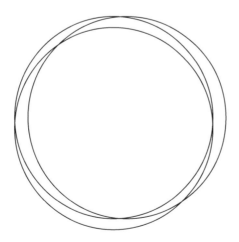

Moses Leads God's People – But Not Easily

Before we get to the meat of this series of lessons, several important events have taken place that are beyond the scope of this study. After his encounter with God at the Burning Bush, Moses obediently (albeit reluctantly) goes back to Egypt and confronts Pharaoh, demanding that Pharaoh let God's people go. God displays His magnificent power over Pharaoh and all of Egypt's gods with 10 plagues: after the last—which holds the birth of Passover, when the oldest child in every Egyptian home is taken by the angel of death—Pharaoh releases the Hebrews. After miraculously crossing the Red Sea, God's people are free from Egypt.

By this point in the story of The Exodus out of Egypt, God's people have *heard* the Ten Commandments (chapter 20). They know God is leading them [pillar of fire at night, pillar of cloud by day] and have seen His miracles along the way [ten plagues, crossing the Red Sea, water, manna, and quail]. Now, God calls Moses up onto Mt. Sinai again to receive a written copy of the Ten Commandments along with many other statutes regarding life as His people. The LORD is now teaching His people what it means to live in relationship with Him.

The Children of Israel now sit at the base of Mt. Sinai. God now calls Moses, who goes up the mountain to meet with Him.

Exodus 24:15–18 *(ESV)*

15Then Moses went up on the mountain, and the cloud covered the mountain. 16The glory of the Lord dwelt on Mount Sinai, and the cloud covered it <u>six days. And on the seventh day he called to Moses</u> out of the midst of the cloud. 17Now the appearance of the glory of the Lord was like a devouring fire on the top of the mountain in the sight of the people of Israel. 18Moses entered the cloud and went up on the mountain. And Moses was on the mountain forty days and forty nights.

Moses waits on God for six days before the interaction begins. Those six days of silence (and possibly fasting) hold interesting connotations. This time of waiting was probably quite important in his faith development. By this point in Moses' story, he's been to the burning bush, dealt with the 10 Plagues and the hard-heartedness of Pharaoh. He's miraculously crossed the Red Sea, seen fresh water pour from a rock, and seen God's provision for a couple million people. God is real to Moses. Now comes the challenge of patience. We're about to see the mysterious and the angry side of God.

First, Moses has to sit and wait for God for six days. Let's take a few moments and examine our own responses to waiting on God. Psalm 13 can be helpful in moving us along that path. On the next page, the psalm has been broken out into instructional pieces. The path of this particular prayer is helpful, as it moves us from despairing about a situation into embracing God's will and way. Read through each section of the psalm and respond to the questions in the boxes. There's plenty of room around the verses to write your thoughts or draw something that represents how you deal with these ideas.

After you have completed this process (found on the next page), share what you have learned with your group.

Close with prayer.

Psalm 13

¹How long, O Lord? Will you forget me forever?
How long will you hide your face from me?
²How long must I take counsel in my soul and
have sorrow in my heart all the day?
How long shall my enemy be exalted over me?

Question God
Go ahead - God can take your questions.
Are you able to wait patiently for God to
act in your life? Or are you a toe-tapper?
What is your go-to response to waiting?

Talk it over with God
God WANTS to hear from you. How long
does it take you to lift up your situation
to God? Is that time of prayer comforting
or a struggle?

³Consider and answer me, O Lord my God; light
up my eyes, lest I sleep the sleep of death,
⁴lest my enemy say, "I have prevailed over him,"
lest my foes rejoice because I am shaken.

Learn to Trust
No matter how things look, we trust.
Trust is earned. Has God earned your
trust? How?

⁵But I have trusted in your steadfast love;

Worship God - No Matter What
Because God is worthy! What is your
go-to worship practice? What brings
you the most comfort and knowledge of
God's presence?

my heart shall rejoice in your salvation. ⁶I will
sing to the Lord,

Receive What God Brings
Because there will always be something.
God always provides whatever we need
in the moment. Can you think of some-
thing unexpected you've received from
God during a trial?

because he has dealt bountifully with me.

Unit Four

When the Crowd Presses In

Open with prayer.

Dear Lord God, in Your great love for us, You have given us Your Word. Be welcome during our time of study, that Your truths may inhabit our hearts and minds. Pour out inspiration, insight, and even challenge as we engage with You in conversation through the gift of the Bible. Open our hearts and minds so that we may hear Your voice. In the name of our Savior, Jesus, we pray. Amen.

Opening Activity

Have you ever been caught "red-handed" doing something you aren't supposed to do? [I know of a woman who made a pie in the morning and then proceeded to eat the entire pie throughout the day, one sliver at a time. The family did not have pie for dessert that night. And no, it wasn't me.] Think back for a few moments and then share (whatever you're comfortable sharing) with your group, or jot down a few notes about that incident in your life.

Moses Returns to the People

Imagine being allowed into God's presence for forty days. One can only speculate about what that experience was like for Moses, but from what we know of God, it was life changing. During those forty days, Moses received a written version of the Ten Commandments along with instructions for life as God's people. Moses returned to The Children of Israel, only to find that they have descended into idolatry and chaos.

Exodus 32:1–6 *(ESV)*

[1]When the people saw that Moses delayed to come down from the mountain, <u>the people gathered themselves together to Aaron</u> and said to him, "Up, make us gods who shall go before us. As for this Moses, the man who brought us up out of the land of Egypt, we do not know what has become of him." [2]So Aaron said to them, "Take off the rings of gold that are in the ears of your wives, your sons, and your daughters, and bring them to me." [3]So all the people took off the rings of gold that were in their ears and brought them to Aaron. [4]And he received the gold from their hand and fashioned it with a graving tool and made a golden calf. And they said, "These are your gods, O Israel, who brought you up out of the land of Egypt!" [5]When Aaron saw this, he built an altar before it. And Aaron made a proclamation and said, "Tomorrow shall be a feast to the Lord." [6]And they rose up early the next day and offered burnt offerings and brought peace offerings. And the people sat down to eat and drink and rose up to play.

There is some ambiguity among Hebrew scholars/translators as to which preposition to use in reference to what takes place between Aaron and the people. "The people gathered themselves together *around/against/about Aaron*". All other instances of this particular preposition in the Old Testament lean into "against", indicating that the people were staging an uprising against Aaron, and he was in danger. He feared for his safety, or popularity, or acceptance.

Discussion Question:

Even though Aaron knew better, he mistakenly allowed the presence and opinion of the crowd to guide his decision. How do you respond? *(Read Proverbs 9:10; 1:7; Psalm 111:10)*

_____

_____

_____

_____

**Watch video #13 "Digital Witness - #1 Cultural Challenges to our Digital Witness"
by Dr. Chad Lakies that accompanies this lesson at
Visual Faith™ Ministry: Movable Adventure Bible Study
visualfaithmin.org/movablebiblestudy**
This video is 45 minutes, so you may wish to make this video a lesson by itself.

This story is brutally honest about the human condition.

1. We are fickle.
2. We are impatient.
3. We are short-sighted.
4. We carry a "what have You done for me lately" attitude.
5. The people had been under Egyptian influence for their entire lives. They may have left Egypt, but Egypt still lived within them.

WE ARE NOT IMMUNE TO ANY OF THESE SAME FAILINGS.

We may not live in Egypt, but we would be wise to regularly ponder how our surroundings are impacting our lives. The Golden Calf is an image of our own desire to control God, making it idolatry in its purest form. It's what Satan used to tempt Adam and Eve when he said, "you will be like God".

Genesis 3:1–6 *(ESV)*

¹Now the serpent was more crafty than any other beast of the field that the Lord God had made. He said to the woman, "Did God actually say, 'You shall not eat of any tree in the garden'?" ²And the woman said to the serpent, "We may eat of the fruit of the trees in the garden, ³but God said, 'You shall not eat of the fruit of the tree that is in the midst of the garden, neither shall you touch it, lest you die.'" ⁴But the serpent said to the woman, "You will not surely die. ⁵For God knows that when you eat of it your eyes will be opened, and you will be like God, knowing good and evil." ⁶So when the woman saw that the tree was good for food, and that it was a delight to the eyes, and that the tree was to be desired to make one wise, she took of its fruit and ate, and she also gave some to her husband who was with her, and he ate.

Examining the details

One of the first things the Israelites do is disparage the character of Moses. He has been chosen by God to lead them out of captivity and slavery. And yet, after he's been up on the mountain with God for only forty days, they turn against him. Aaron stands as their cudgel. They call their leader "that man Moses". They are implying that Moses (and by association, God Himself) has abandoned them. And so they speak of Moses with total disrespect. We often abandon our spiritual leaders because we are more impressed by our own opinions. Especially in the U.S., personal opinion trumps all other ideas. Some of us have been brought up to believe in our own "rightness". Like the Israelites' golden calf, this is also idolatry in its purest form. These are perhaps rather provocative words. But some examination of our own fervently held ideas is always a wise path.

Discussion Questions:

Have we disrespected those whom God has set over us as our spiritual leaders (Pastors, Elders, Parents)? Have you seen personally or in the life of another, how reliance on self or following a false leader has been damaging? How so, and specifically how so in the Christian life? Or perhaps we have set ourselves at the feet of someone who doesn't truly know God and His Word. How does that play out in the Christian's life? How might that be damaging?

God doesn't leave us adrift in these matters. He gives us, through the Holy Spirit, the gift of discernment. *[Discernment: The ability to perceive good/evil, right/wrong correctly. For the Christian, this happens through the power and guidance of the Holy Spirit.]* God doesn't want us to wander and wonder if we're on the right path. Righteous wisdom is stronger in those who seek God. If you ask for wisdom, He will grant it. (see James 1:5) The Old Testament prophets advised the same.

Hosea 14:9 *(ESV)*

Whoever is wise, let him understand these things; whoever is discerning, let him know them; for the ways of the Lord are right, and the upright walk in them, but transgressors stumble in them.

FOR the WAYS OF the LORD ARE RIGHT.

Hosea 14:9

Discussion Questions:

As humans we want to be confident and find people in which we can put our trust. Where do you look and how do you decide among the various options? How do you discern what is best?

_____

_____

_____

_____

In 1 Kings 3:16–28 is another excellent Biblical example of discernment in one of God's leaders. When you read stories like this, what do they do to your faith? Your spirit? Your walk with God?

_____

_____

_____

_____

Close with prayer.

Movable

PATHWAYS FOR TRANSFORMATION
A VISUAL FAITH EVENT NOV 2021

If Some one could see you, what would they say you're trying to do?

Living on Autopilot

our habits = ourselves

our Digital Witness MATTERS

- ✓ On line disInhibition EFFECT → Treating People worse on line
- ✓ OUTRAGE INDUSTRIAL complex
  - ↳ Mechanical generation that is
    - Angry and out raged
    - contempt

→ Does this impact our face to face

4 CHALLENGES

1. IDEological Differences - Ties that Bind VS BLIND
2. Reacting before understanding
3. Assuming MOTIVATION
4. Antagonism shapes perceptions

Accidental Courtesy

Intellectual Humility → CHARACTER ←

Chad Lakies - #1 cultural challenges to our digital witness

@BLESSINKS

SKETCHNOTED BY: MARSHA BAKER

My Sketchnotes

Unit Four

Personal Idols

Open with prayer.

Using the illustration of the golden calf below spend some time in personal confession. Todays lesson examines the idolatry of the Children of Israel. We can never read theses stories without seeing ourselves. On the "calf" idol below, jot down some of the things that may have taken on the role of idol in your life. Clearly, we don't bow down to golden calves anymore. But, we all have things that take the place of God (at times) in our lives. Think about the things/people/situations that might have a place in your life that might be less than ideal. Seek God's forgiveness for those moment of idolatry.

Syncretism and the Worship of a Golden Calf

Aaron instructs the people to remove the gold jewelry they are wearing and bring it to him, that an idol might be constructed. It seems odd that they would possess gold and silver jewelry, since they had been mere slaves in Egypt. But, as the Children of Israel fled Egypt after the Passover (The Last Plague), the Egyptians gave them all kinds of jewelry and clothing. According to Rabbinic tradition, much of this jewelry could have had implications for the cultic worship of the Egyptians.

Exodus 12:33–36 (ESV)

³³ *The Egyptians were urgent with the people to send them out of the land in haste. For they said, "We shall all be dead."* ³⁴ *So the people took their dough before it was leavened, their kneading bowls being bound up in their cloaks on their shoulders.* ³⁵ *The people of Israel had also done as Moses told them, for they had asked the Egyptians for silver and gold jewelry and for clothing.* ³⁶ *And the Lord had given the people favor in the sight of the Egyptians, so that they let them have what they asked. Thus they plundered the Egyptians.*

We cannot assume the Children of Israel have given up their faith in God entirely. What they have chosen instead is an amalgamation of what they learned in Egypt and what they know from their history about God. This is called *syncretism*. Whenever we mix faith in the True and Living God with *anything* else, we are guilty of creating our own god. If you read your Bible everyday but then also dwell in the world of astrology, you have created your own god. If you worship the Lord on Sunday and then practice eastern mysticism on Monday, you have created your own god. Any time you say (or think), "No god of mine would ...", you've created your own god. You see where this is going. Idolatry is a subtle and enormous trap. Satan loves it and God hates it. In Exodus 32:5, we see God's people create what they call "a feast to the LORD". As they mix the worship of Yahweh with bowing down to a golden calf, they have nullified their spiritual lives. This story is recounted by Nehemiah and the Children of Israel do not look good in the retelling.

Nehemiah 9:16–19 (ESV)

¹⁶ *"But they and our fathers acted presumptuously and stiffened their neck and did not obey your commandments.* ¹⁷ *They refused to obey and were not mindful of the wonders that you performed among them, but they stiffened their neck and appointed a leader to return to their slavery in Egypt. But you are a God ready to forgive, gracious and merciful, slow to anger and abounding in steadfast love, and did not forsake them.* ¹⁸ *Even when they had made for themselves a golden calf and said, 'This is your God who brought you up out of Egypt,' and had committed great blasphemies,* ¹⁹ *you in your great mercies did not forsake them in the wilderness. The pillar of cloud to lead them in the way did not depart from them by day, nor the pillar of fire by night to light for them the way by which they should go.*

And yet, God continues to stick with them, despite the fact that they throw a party and engage in orgies. Nowhere in Scripture does God offer up the party lifestyle for His people. God is not pleased with idol worship and licentious parties.

Discussion Question:

Our culture is filled with ideas and religions that attempt to "mix" with Christianity. Can you think of any such ideas? (Just to get you started – The Long Island Medium, Astrology, ...)

Exodus 32:7–10 *(ESV)*

[7]And the LORD said to Moses, "Go down, for your people, whom you brought up out of the land of Egypt, have corrupted themselves. [8]They have turned aside quickly out of the way that I commanded them. They have made for themselves a golden calf and have worshiped it and sacrificed to it and said, 'These are your gods, O Israel, who brought you up out of the land of Egypt!'" [9]And the LORD said to Moses, "I have seen this people, and behold, it is a stiff-necked people. [10]Now therefore let me alone, that my wrath may burn hot against them and I may consume them, in order that I may make a great nation of you."

While Moses sits with God on top of Mt. Sinai, the people party below. Moses knows nothing of what is going on at the base of the mountain, but God knows it all. We must keep God's character in mind throughout the next few verses. The actions of the people are not unexpected by God. We can never visualize God striking his forehead with His palm and saying, "I didn't see that coming!" God has never and will never be in that position. No, He knew the people would abandon Him (and Moses). He knew that they would get caught up in vile idolatry. And His reactions seem to be appropriate. He declares them to be "Moses' people". He appears to turn His back on them. He rightfully calls them "stiff-necked". This term is taken from the experience of working with animals on a farm. It means they are being willfully obstinate. Work animals will stiffen their necks and refuse to do as they are commanded. (Or perhaps you've picked up a toddler to demand compliance with something only to have them suddenly completely relax their shoulders, and thus they slip back onto the ground. They do that for the same reason the oxen will stiffen his neck. Willful obstinance.)

There are several stories in the Bible that might inspire us to say "wow" every single time we read them. The recounting of the golden calf is just such a story. We are appalled at Aaron's incredible lack of leadership and faithfulness and stunned by Moses' willingness to intercede for this feckless people. There are also feelings of surprise at the actions of the people. Moses is gone on the mountain for only forty days and the people devise an idol to worship. The most shocking of all is the undeserved grace that God shows to the people who show Him utter disrespect and disregard.

But we shouldn't be surprised. Our own lives are filled with examples of sinful disrespect and disregard. It often takes us far less than forty days to betray God. In this story we find an absolutely honest look at God and the fact that our sin does indeed affect Him. He is hurt and angered by the people and their golden idol. He has specifically told them not to take part in that very activity and now here they are, building a golden calf. Of course His anger burns.

Let's Examine God's Response

What we see in God at this point is righteous anger brought on by the fact that the defection of His people hurts. Yes, God is hurt. Let's draw in closer. If you've ever raised children, you know what it's like to be hurt by your child. They make decisions that are unwise, foolish, and sometimes dangerous. As parents, we're hurt by those events. Often, we would use the word disappointed which tends to display itself as anger. Disappointment happens when our expectations are dashed, and anger is the result. But God has never been disappointed with us, because He is omnipotent (He knows all). He is never surprised by our actions or decisions. His expectations are always 100% accurate. Disappointment is not a word we can use about how God feels about us. But He can be and is hurt by our disobedience—every time. Many have struggled in their relationship with God because they believe they are a disappointment to Him. They know they cannot be perfect, and they believe that's what He expects.

Discussion Questions:

Have you ever hurt God with your disobedience? How do you deal with that and what impact does that have on your relationship with Him?

Have you ever been disappointed with God (your expectations didn't match reality)? What impact have those feelings had on your relationship with Him?

How does God deal with you when you hurt Him or feel disappointed in Him? The right answer is Jesus—just like in Sunday School—but articulating that belief is critical. Spend some time, in any way that best speaks for you, sharing your saving faith in Jesus. If you don't truly know that Jesus is your Savior, speak to someone who does. It will be life changing conversation.

Watch video #14 "Digital Witness - #2 Following Jesus Online: The Shape of Digital Witness"
by Dr. Chad Lakies that accompanies this lesson at
Visual Faith™ Ministry: Movable Adventure Bible Study
visualfaithmin.org/movablebiblestudy
This video is 45 minutes, so you may wish to make this video a lesson by itself.

Close with prayer.

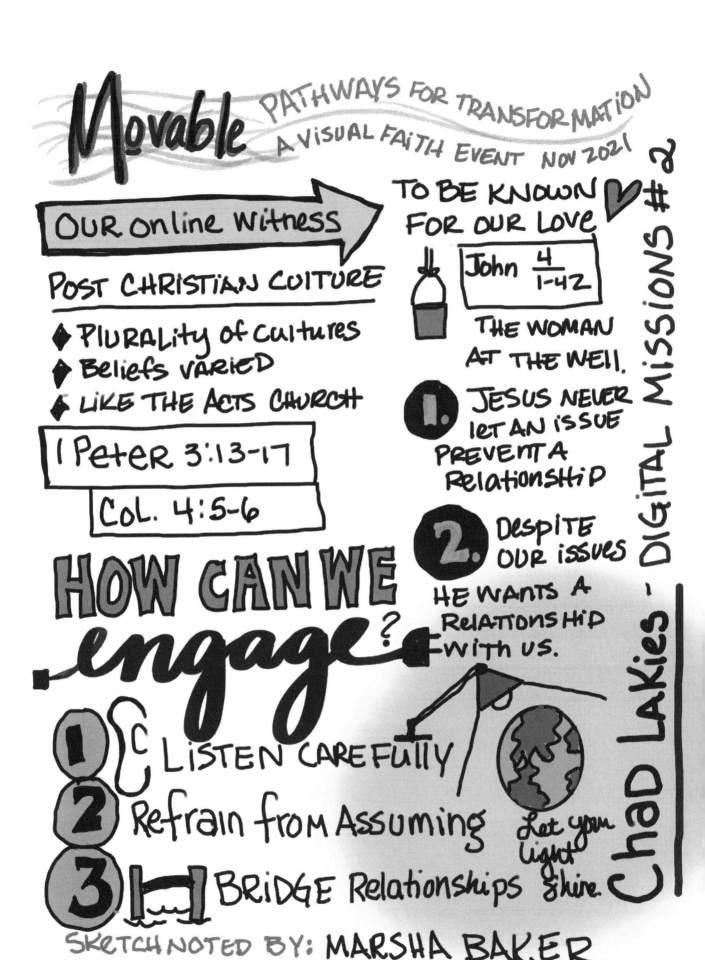

Movable PATHWAYS FOR TRANSFORMATION
A VISUAL FAITH EVENT NOV 2021

OUR online Witness

TO BE KNOWN FOR OUR LOVE

John 4 1-42

THE WOMAN AT THE WELL.

POST CHRISTIAN CULTURE
- PLURALITY of Cultures
- Beliefs VARIED
- LIKE THE ACTS CHURCH

1 Peter 3:13-17

Col. 4:5-6

1. JESUS NEVER let AN ISSUE PREVENT A Relationship

2. Despite OUR issues HE WANTS A RELATIONSHIP WITH US.

HOW CAN WE engage?

1 LISTEN CAREFULLY

2 Refrain from Assuming

3 BRIDGE Relationships   Let your light shine.

Chad Lakies - DIGITAL MISSIONS # 2

SKETCH NOTED BY: MARSHA BAKER

My Sketchnotes

Unit Four

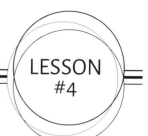
When Idols Emerge

Open with prayer.

Dear Lord, we are grateful for the stories of Your people who lived lives just like ours with struggles and joys, successes and disappointments. They mirror the kinds of things we face, and we are informed as to how to better face them with You in mind. Continue that good work in us as we examine how we live and allow You to make changes in our spirits that will deepen our faith and make us more mindful of how we live. In Jesus' name we pray. Amen.

Opening Activity

What kinds of situations cause you to lose patience with God, with those around you, or yourself? What are your "pet peeves"? Share your answers with your group.

....

....

....

....

Moses is *Moved*

Moses has been leading the people for a few months at this point. We have watched the events of his life since his birth. He was raised with wealth, although separated from his true family. He takes matters into his own hands at the age of 40 and kills an Egyptian who is beating a Hebrew. After running for his life, he lives in Midian for forty years, creating a life and family for himself. God grabs Moses at the age of 80 and brings him back to Egypt as his spokesman and leader of God's people. Now it appears God is going to abandon this group of people and start over with Moses as the father of a "new people". But Moses has grown. He has changed and matured. God's words "let me alone" are seen by Moses as an invitation to intercede for the people. He speaks boldly, albeit respectfully, to God, reminding Him who He is and what He has promised His people. Remarkably, this is only the first of several times when Moses will intercede with God for the people.

Reference	Event
Numbers 11:1-2	The people "complained about their misfortunes"
Numbers 12:1-13	Miriam (Moses' sister) attacks Moses and God deals with her
Numbers 14:1-19	The people grumble against Moses and Aaron – again
Numbers 16:1-35	The sons of Korah bring down God's wrath
Numbers 21:4-9	The people become impatient – again – and speak against God and Moses

Skim over the stories on the previous page. Note the similarities in the stories. What is the overriding character of each event? What do we learn about Moses' leadership of God's people? What do we learn about God and how He deals with us?

Moses invites God to "remember"

> **Remembered:** The Hebrew stem *z-k-r* connotes much more than the recall of things past. It means, rather, to be mindful, to pay heed, signifying a sharp focusing of attention upon someone or something. It embraces concern and involvement and is active not passive, so that it eventuates in action. "Looking upon leads to remembering and remembering leads to action."
>
> Sarna, N. M. ©1991. *Exodus* (p. 13). Philadelphia: Jewish Publication Society

Moses steps into the role of leader at this point in the story and intercedes for the people. God hears Moses. God acts on Moses' intercession. This is an interesting interaction, similar to the one between Abraham and God over the cities of Sodom and Gomorrah (See Genesis 18:16–33). He even tells God that He will look bad in the eyes of their enemies (the Egyptians) if He now destroys the people He has rescued from slavery. Here we see the evidence of the real relationship that has been forged between God and Moses. Moses is free to speak with honesty to the Lord of the Universe. That should inspire us to do the same. Most shocking at this point in the story is that God hears Moses' words and does not destroy the people. God always chooses grace first. God does the same thing for us every single day for we deserve destruction and yet don't receive it because of the blood of Jesus. Grace is the overriding aspect of God's story once again.

Discussion Questions:

Is God's mind changed or is He simply exercising relationship? Who is MOVED in this situation?

Exodus 32:11–14 *(ESV)*

[11]*But Moses implored the LORD his God and said, "O LORD, why does your wrath burn hot against your people, whom you have brought out of the land of Egypt with great power and with a mighty hand?* [12]*Why should the Egyptians say, 'With evil intent did he bring them out, to kill them in the mountains and to consume them from the face of the earth'? Turn from your burning anger and relent from this disaster against your people.* [13]*Remember Abraham, Isaac, and Israel, your servants, to whom you swore by your own self, and said to them, 'I will multiply your offspring as the stars of heaven, and all this land that I have promised I will give to your offspring, and they shall inherit it forever.'"* [14]*And the LORD relented from the disaster that he had spoken of bringing on his people.*

Suddenly, we are looking at a new Moses. He has been transformed from a spoiled prince into a true, compassionate leader. He seeks God's face for *mercy* for the people.

His prayer is:

- Compelling
- Truthful
- Mindful of the past

From God's response to this request, as given in 34:6–7, it is clear that Moses here asks to comprehend God's essential personality, the attributes that guide His actions in His dealings with humankind, the norms by which He operates in His governance of the world. This understanding of what is meant by "the ways of God" is corroborated by Psalm 103:7–8, the earliest extant commentary on this text: "He made known His ways to Moses,/His deeds to the children of Israel,/The LORD is compassionate and gracious,/slow to anger, abounding in steadfast love." Moses' request, like the assertion of Abraham before him— "Shall not the Judge of all the earth deal justly?"—rests on the postulate that God is not capricious but acts according to norms that human beings can try to understand.

Sarna, N. M. ©1991. *Exodus* (p. 213). Philadelphia: Jewish Publication Society.

Moses Asks God to Temper His Anger, But Moses ...

Exodus 32:15–24 *(ESV)*

15 Then Moses turned and went down from the mountain with the two tablets of the testimony in his hand, tablets that were written on both sides; on the front and on the back they were written. 16 The tablets were the work of God, and the writing was the writing of God, engraved on the tablets. 17 When Joshua heard the noise of the people as they shouted, he said to Moses, "There is a noise of war in the camp." 18 But he said, "It is not the sound of shouting for victory, or the sound of the cry of defeat, but the sound of singing that I hear." 19 And as soon as he came near the camp and saw the calf and the dancing, Moses' anger burned hot, and he threw the tablets out of his hands and broke them at the foot of the mountain. 20 He took the calf that they had made and burned it with fire and ground it to powder and scattered it on the water and made the people of Israel drink it. 21 And Moses said to Aaron, "What did this people do to you that you have brought such a great sin upon them?" 22 And Aaron said, "Let not the anger of my LORD burn hot. You know the people, that they are set on evil. 23 For they said to me, 'Make us gods who shall go before us. As for this Moses, the man who brought us up out of the land of Egypt, we do not know what has become of him.' 24 So I said to them, 'Let any who have gold take it off.' So they gave it to me, and I threw it into the fire, and out came this calf."

Discussion Questions:

As you read this story, can you visualize two old guys (Moses and Aaron are both over 80 at this point) standing before a golden calf and having this discussion? What would you say if you were Moses? What would you feel if you were Aaron?

This scene between Moses and Aaron is one of the most perplexing conversations in the Bible. Aaron's words to Moses after he crafts the golden calf for the people seem ridiculous. *"So they gave it [the gold] to me, and I threw it into the fire, and out came this calf."* Aaron's excuse defies logic. Moses has no reply for this excuse, because really — what could you possibly say to something like that?

Before this almost comical conversation, we see Moses actually destroy the stone tablets that bear the Ten Commandments written by the hand of God Himself! That's some serious anger right there. (God makes Moses pay for that choice later.) But we can't blame Moses for his anger. The people have lost their spiritual center. And their temporary leader has not helped with the situation. Aaron could have made so many other choices when presented with the complaints of the people. Instead he gives into their idolatrous desires and creates an idol for them to worship. Moses' response is immediate and violent. He grinds up the idol and sprinkles it into the water supply. Now the people must consume their new "god". There is also retribution in the form of death as several people are killed by the sword wielded by the Levites. Three-thousand people lose their lives that day. The price of idolatry is high.

A few questions arise in connection with this brief account that are not fully answered in the Bible itself. Why did Moses make the people drink the water mixed with the material of the golden calf? Was this to demonstrate to the people how weak their idol-god was? Did he want to humiliate them by having them drink a god whom they had worshiped? Was this a punishment to show that they had desecrated their only true source of life, just as water is a source of life? Was a result of this drinking the plague mentioned in verse 35, which the Lord caused to come upon the people? Was this simply the result of Moses' burning anger, without any special meaning attached to it? The Bible doesn't say. There may be some truth in all of the above opinions, which have been expressed by Bible scholars.

Wendland, E. H. ©2000. *Exodus* (p. 208). Milwaukee, WI: Northwestern Pub. House.

Finally, we find Moses returning to the Lord and interceding for the people. They most certainly didn't deserve it, but Moses is a great leader and surprisingly offers himself up as a sacrifice for their sinfulness (See Exodus 32:32). God does not accept this offer as Moses is not the Messiah and is sinful himself. His sacrifice would not pay the price for their sin. The Apostle Paul makes a similar offer in the book of Romans for the Jews who simply refused to believe that Jesus was the Promised Messiah. His offer too is rejected.

 ### Romans 9:3–4 *(ESV)*

³For I could wish that I myself were accursed and cut off from Christ for the sake of my brothers, my kinsmen according to the flesh. ⁴They are Israelites, and to them belong the adoption, the glory, the covenants, the giving of the law, the worship, and the promises.

Psalm 49 notes that while someone might offer up their lives to save many others, their offering is unacceptable. Only the innocent sacrifice of Jesus can pay for our sins.

Psalm 49:7–9 *(ESV)*

⁷Truly no man can ransom another, or give to God the price of his life,

⁸for the ransom of their life is costly and can never suffice,

⁹that he should live on forever and never see the pit.

While God does visit a plague upon the people, He does not destroy them entirely which is what they deserved. He chooses grace *again* and allows them to continue to live as His people. Because of Jesus, God chooses that same course for me and you every single day of our lives. While Moses and Paul may have had it in their hearts to surrender their lives on behalf of the people, they were unfit to do so because of their own sin. Jesus was sinless and thus His sacrifice, made once for all, was the perfect and final payment for my sin. So even in the midst of a rather strange story, we find the Gospel and peace with God.

**Watch video # 15 "When Idols Emerge" that accompanies this lesson at
Visual Faith™ Ministry: Movable Adventure Bible Study
visualfaithmin.org/movablebiblestudy**

Close with prayer.

My Sketchnotes

Unit Four

LESSON #5

Moses "Sees" God

 **Open with prayer.**

Thank You, dear Lord, for Your great love and kindness to us throughout this study. Thank You for lessons to learn, transformation to embrace, and friends with which to share it. Come into this last lesson and draw us ever closer to You. Fill us with the knowledge of Your presence, and shine Your love through us, that we might share You with others. In Jesus' name we pray. Amen.

Opening Activity

What have you learned over the last few weeks of this series? Have you noticed any transformations in your thinking, behaviors, or attitudes? How has God worked in you throughout this process?

God Responds / Moses Responds

In response to His great anger over the golden calf, God says He will withdraw His presence from the Children of Israel and send instead an angel to lead the people. He does this because He is a God of grace and mercy and doesn't want His anger to lead Him to what the people deserve – their destruction. But this is a dire outcome as far as Moses is concerned. Even the thought of being outside of God's presence is one that brings distress to Moses. Carrying that distress, he addresses his concerns to the Lord. Once again, we are privileged to witness the incredible relationship between God and Moses as they discuss this decision. Because Moses dares to ask God to reconsider His decision to send the angel to lead the people rather than doing it Himself, God does just that. He relents and agrees to set aside His wrath and remain with the people. This reconsideration is taken out of His great love for the people and His deep relationship with Moses. And frankly, Moses plays a little unfairly by claiming that favored place as God's chosen people (*"Is it not in your going with us, so that we are distinct, I and your people, from every other people on the face of the earth"*), thus moving God to agree to stay with the people.

"But," he said, "You cannot see my face, for man shall not see me and live." Ex. 33:20

Exodus 33:12–23 *(ESV)*

¹²Moses said to the Lord, "See, you say to me, 'Bring up this people,' but you have not let me know whom you will send with me. Yet you have said, 'I know you by name, and you have also found favor in my sight.'¹³Now therefore, if I have found favor in your sight, please show me now your ways, that I may know you in order to find favor in your sight. Consider too that this nation is your people." ¹⁴And he said, "My presence will go with you, and I will give you rest." ¹⁵And he said to him, "If your presence will not go with me, do not bring us up from here. ¹⁶For how shall it be known that I have found favor in your sight, I and your people? Is it not in your going with us, so that we are distinct, I and your people, from every other people on the face of the earth?" ¹⁷And the Lord said to Moses, "This very thing that you have spoken I will do, for you have found favor in my sight, and I know you by name." ¹⁸Moses said, "Please show me your glory." ¹⁹And he said, "I will make all my goodness pass before you and will proclaim before you my name 'The Lord.' And I will be gracious to whom I will be gracious, and will show mercy on whom I will show mercy. ²⁰But," he said, "you cannot see my face, for man shall not see me and live." ²¹And the Lord said, "Behold, there is a place by me where you shall stand on the rock, ²²and while my glory passes by I will put you in a cleft of the rock, and I will cover you with my hand until I have passed by. ²³Then I will take away my hand, and you shall see my back, but my face shall not be seen."

After securing God's promise to stay with the people, Moses goes even further. He has spent weeks in God's presence and now has the temerity to ask for even more. *"Show me your glory"* is his next request. If there was ever anyone who had already seen the glory of God, it was Moses and yet he asks for more. Surprisingly, God doesn't chide him for this request but instead honors it in a way that Moses can handle. There is much discussion as to exactly what Moses was allowed to see and the text is largely silent. So we can only assume it was a gift to Moses as He is allowed to experience God's "goodness" to an even larger extent.

God shows me His goodness every single day by providing for all of my needs and seeing me washed in the blood of Jesus Christ. Just as Moses didn't *deserve* to see God's glory, I don't *deserve* the grace I have received and yet God sets aside the wrath I do deserve and gives me grace and forgiveness anyway.

Centuries later, Israel would remember this story and use it during worship to recall their long and gracious relationship with God. Even in the retelling, Moses is central to the story as the one who "stood in the breach" before God, sparing the people from destruction.

Psalm 106:19–23 *(ESV)*

¹⁹They made a calf in Horeb and worshiped a metal image.

²⁰They exchanged the glory of God for the image of an ox that eats grass.

²¹They forgot God, their Savior, who had done great things in Egypt,

²²wondrous works in the land of Ham, and awesome deeds by the Red Sea.

²³Therefore he said he would destroy them—had not Moses, his chosen one, stood in the breach before him, to turn away his wrath from destroying them.

Moses and Jesus

We've touched on a few of the stories of Moses' life. He appears one more time in the Bible after his death and burial by God Himself (Deuteronomy 34:1–8). We find Moses and the prophet Elijah meeting with Jesus on the Mount of Transfiguration. Let's look at that story as it is told in **Mark 9:2–9, 14–29.**

Mark 9:2–9, 14–29 *(ESV)*

²And after six days Jesus took with him Peter and James and John, and led them up a high mountain by themselves. And he was transfigured before them, ³and his clothes became radiant, intensely white, as no one on earth could bleach them. ⁴And there appeared to them Elijah with Moses, and they were talking with Jesus. ⁵And Peter said to Jesus, "Rabbi, it is good that we are here. Let us make three tents, one for you and one for Moses and one for Elijah." ⁶For he did not know what to say, for they were terrified. ⁷And a cloud overshadowed them, and a voice came out of the cloud, "This is my beloved Son; listen to him." ⁸And suddenly, looking around, they no longer saw anyone with them but Jesus only. ⁹And as they were coming down the mountain, he charged them to tell no one what they had seen, until the Son of Man had risen from the dead. ¹⁴And when they came to the disciples, they saw a great crowd around them, and scribes arguing with them. ¹⁵And immediately all the crowd, when they saw him, were greatly amazed and ran up to him and greeted him. ¹⁶And he asked them, "What are you arguing about with them?" ¹⁷And someone from the crowd answered him, "Teacher, I brought my son to you, for he has a spirit that makes him mute. ¹⁸And whenever it seizes him, it throws him down, and he foams and grinds his teeth and becomes rigid. So I asked your disciples to cast it out, and they were not able." ¹⁹And he answered them, "O faithless generation, how long am I to be with you? How long am I to bear with you? Bring him to me." ²⁰And they brought the boy to him. And when the spirit saw him, immediately it convulsed the boy, and he fell on the ground and rolled about, foaming at the mouth. ²¹And Jesus asked his father, "How long has this been happening to him?" And he said, "From childhood. ²²And it has often cast him into fire and into water, to destroy him. But if you can do anything, have compassion on us and help us." ²³And Jesus said to him, "'If you can'! All things are possible for one who believes." ²⁴Immediately the father of the child cried out and said, "I believe; help my unbelief!" ²⁵And when Jesus saw that a crowd came running together, he rebuked the unclean spirit, saying to it, "You mute and deaf spirit, I command you, come out of him and never enter him again." ²⁶And after crying out and convulsing him terribly, it came out, and the boy was like a corpse, so that most of them said, "He is dead." ²⁷But Jesus took him by the hand and lifted him up, and he arose. ²⁸And when he had entered the house, his disciples asked him privately, "Why could we not cast it out?" ²⁹And he said to them, "This kind cannot be driven out by anything but prayer."

As this story unfolds, we find Jesus engaged in an event similar to that of Moses' dealing with an unbelieving people. Moses comes down from a "mountaintop experience" to find a debauched people having a wild party, worshiping an idol created by their own hands. Jesus comes down from meeting with Moses and Elijah on the mountain where God the Father declares His great pleasure with His Son. What does Jesus find when He gets to the to the bottom of the mountain? He finds unbelief on the part of His own disciples. A boy has been tortured by a demon for years and the disciples are unable to cast it out. At least the boy's father is willing to voice his problem when he says, "I believe, help my unbelief."

But we know the difference between Moses and Jesus. Moses was a sinful human. Jesus is the Son of God. Moses' role was as leader of a captive people that God chose to free. Moses spent forty years leading the people around the wilderness. (The whole story of the reason for those forty years of wandering can be found in **Numbers 13 & 14**.) But he died just like everyone else. He had no solution for our greatest problem—we are sinners in need of a Savior. Jesus is the answer to that problem. His sacrificial death on the cross paid the price for all our sin. Because of the shedding of His innocent blood, we are holy in the eyes of a Holy God. Moses won freedom from slavery in Egypt for God's people. Jesus won freedom from slavery to sin for all who would believe. Moses grew, changed, and was transformed by God for the work that needed to be done.

Discussion Questions:

What work does God have for you to do? How might He need to equip you to serve those around you in His name?

What kinds of practices might be helpful in moving you deeper into God's will and presence in your life? How might you cooperate with those changes?

Watch video #16 "Moses 'Sees' God" that accompanies this lesson at
Visual Faith™ Ministry: Movable Adventure Bible Study
visualfaithmin.org/movablebiblestudy

Close with prayer.

Read together Psalm 51. This is the Psalm that King David wrote after his sin with Bathsheba. Read it aloud verse by verse as printed below. Embrace the confession that is the thrust of this prayer.

[1]*Have mercy on me, O God, according to your steadfast love; according to your abundant mercy blot out my transgressions.*

[2]*Wash me thoroughly from my iniquity, and cleanse me from my sin!*

[3]*For I know my transgressions, and my sin is ever before me.*

[4]*Against you, you only, have I sinned and done what is evil in your sight, so that you may be justified in your words and blameless in your judgment.*

[5]*Behold, I was brought forth in iniquity, and in sin did my mother conceive me.*

[6]*Behold, you delight in truth in the inward being, and you teach me wisdom in the secret heart.*

[7]*Purge me with hyssop, and I shall be clean; wash me, and I shall be whiter than snow.*

[8]*Let me hear joy and gladness; let the bones that you have broken rejoice.*

[9]*Hide your face from my sins, and blot out all my iniquities.*

[10]*Create in me a clean heart, O God, and renew a right spirit within me.*

[11]*Cast me not away from your presence, and take not your Holy Spirit from me.*

[12]*Restore to me the joy of your salvation, and uphold me with a willing spirit.*

[13]*Then I will teach transgressors your ways, and sinners will return to you.*

[14]*Deliver me from bloodguiltiness, O God, O God of my salvation, and my tongue will sing aloud of your righteousness.*

[15]*O Lord, open my lips, and my mouth will declare your praise.*

[16]*For you will not delight in sacrifice, or I would give it; you will not be pleased with a burnt offering.*

[17]*The sacrifices of God are a broken spirit; a broken and contrite heart, O God, you will not despise.*

[18]*Do good to Zion in your good pleasure; build up the walls of Jerusalem;*

[19]*then will you delight in right sacrifices, in burnt offerings and whole burnt offerings; then bulls will be offered on your altar.*

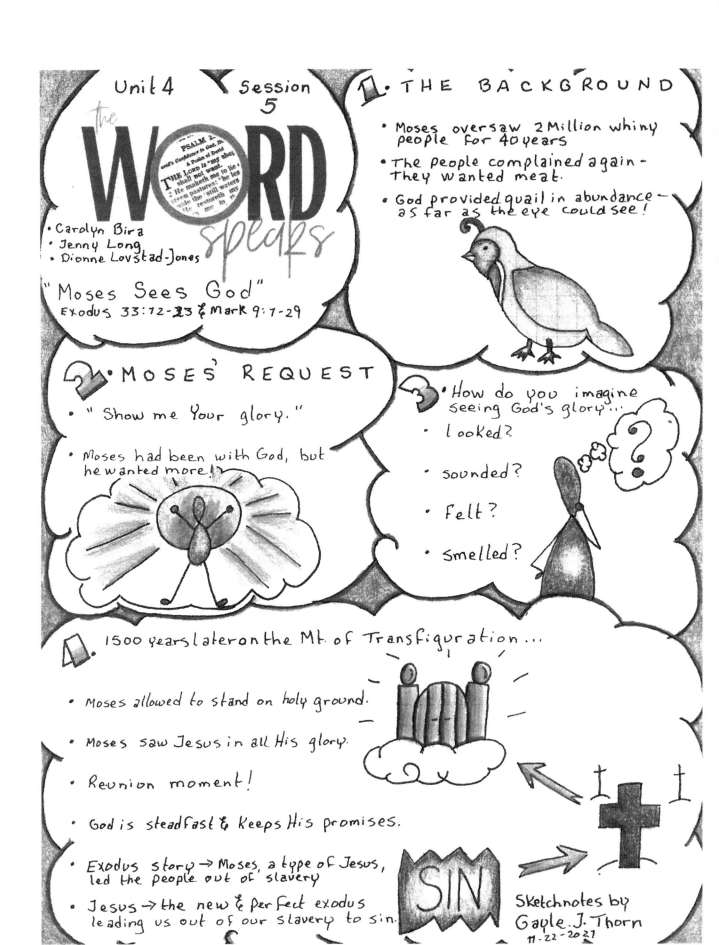

Unit 4 — Session 5

the WORD speaks

PSALM 23
A Psalm of David
THE LORD is my shep... shall not want.
2 He maketh me to lie... green pastures; he lea... side the still waters.
3 He restoreth my...

- Carolyn Bira
- Jenny Long
- Dionne Lovstad-Jones

"Moses Sees God"
Exodus 33:12-23 & Mark 9:7-29

1. THE BACKGROUND

- Moses oversaw 2 Million whiny people for 40 years
- The people complained again - they wanted meat.
- God provided quail in abundance - as far as the eye could see!

2. MOSES' REQUEST

- "Show me Your glory."
- Moses had been with God, but he wanted more!

3.
- How do you imagine seeing God's glory...
  - looked?
  - sounded?
  - felt?
  - smelled?

4. 1500 years later on the Mt. of Transfiguration...

- Moses allowed to stand on holy ground.
- Moses saw Jesus in all His glory.
- Reunion moment!
- God is steadfast & keeps His promises.
- Exodus story → Moses, a type of Jesus, led the people out of slavery
- Jesus → the new & perfect exodus leading us out of our slavery to sin.

SIN

Sketchnotes by
Gayle J. Thorn
11-22-2021

120

My Sketchnotes

Lingering Over His Word

We are happy to provide several visual faith components for you to use and experience.

     Directions (colored version is available to view at *visualfaithmin.org/movablebiblestudy*)
     Lined Notebook Paper Printable
     How to Bind a Journal Videos found at *visualfaithmin.org/movablebiblestudy*)
          3 Hole Binding by Denise Miller
          5 Hole Binding by Candice Schwark

     Directions
     Example page
     Playful Fonts Samples
     Five Blank Templates (straight, wavy, mountain, path, flower mixed lines)

     Directions
     Example page
     Blank page for you to try it out.

     Directions (colored version is available to view at *visualfaithmin.org/movablebiblestudy*)
     Final image (colored version is available to view at *visualfaithmin.org/movablebiblestudy*)
     How to Video can be found at *visualfaithmin.org/movablebiblestudy*

     Examples Page
     May I Be Transformed Mixed Media Project Directions
     Video by Denise Miller can be found at *visualfaithmin.org/movablebiblestudy*
     Conformed to Transform Mixed Media Project Directions
     Word Art
     Video by Candice Schwark can be found at *visualfaithmin.org/movablebiblestudy*

Lingering Over His Word
Using Creative Techniques

HANDMADE JOURNAL for scripture writing prayers, etc.

Using 3 or 5-hole Pamphlet binding

3. Group six to eight sheets of 8.5" x 11" paper and fold to 8.5" x 5.11" (copy/lined/graph/dot paper or a variety of each)

Insert into cover. Trim edges if necessary.

Mark top of each page including cover with a T so you keep them all in order (erase T later)

1. Buy colorful file folders, or recycle a used one, and embellish with colorful papers, paints, etc.

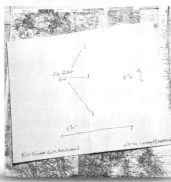

2. Trim file folder to 8-3/4" x 11-1/2" take advantage of the folder's scored fold - make a template of that to use for a future journal. Fold in half.

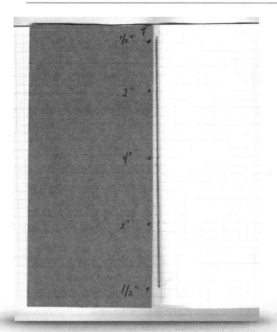

6. Use waxed thread, embroidery floss, or even waxed dental floss, and a needle that fits easily through the holes (not too big of an eye).

Follow sewing guide numbers. If you start on the inside center hole, the tails will be on the inside.

If you start on the outside center hole, they will be on the outside for adding beads, etc.

4. Make a strip of card stock that is the same height as the page inserts (signature), Mark from top at 1/2", 2" , 4" and 1/2" from bottom. Mark holes on inside of signature (according to stitches you want to do. 1/2", 4" and 1/2' from bottom for 3-hole. Use all holes for 5-hole pattern.

5. Center the signature inside the cover, clip together on both sides and punch holes through all pages and cover, being careful to keep your holes on the fold. When done, follow sewing instructions.

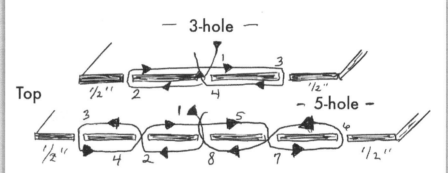

Starting inside book center hole....trim thread tie off with square knot and smooth thread ends

7. Add pockets to the inside covers

Creative Writing Instructions

By Denise Miller

1. Choose a page from the 5 provided.

2. Either write directly in this book or make a copy.

3. Write out a favorite Bible verse from the Bible study.

4. Use your normal handwriting or try a fun font or even try a different font per word (Playful Fonts page is included to give some ideas).

5. Add color or doodles or leave black and white.

6. Example page (below right) shows a different font per word, letters mostly touching top and bottom of each line, and doodles.

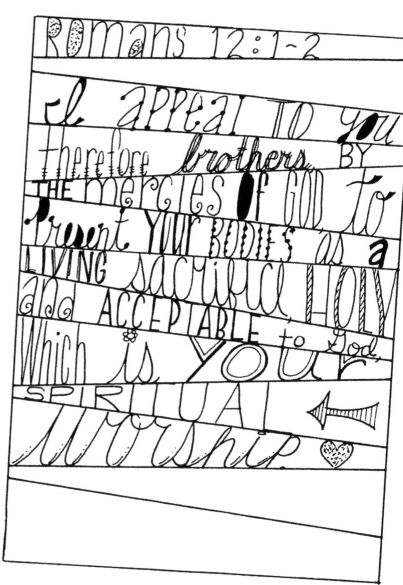

Playful fonts:
LOVE love love
love LOVE Love
LOVE love LOVE
Love Love love
Love Love LOVE
LoVe love Love
LOVE Love

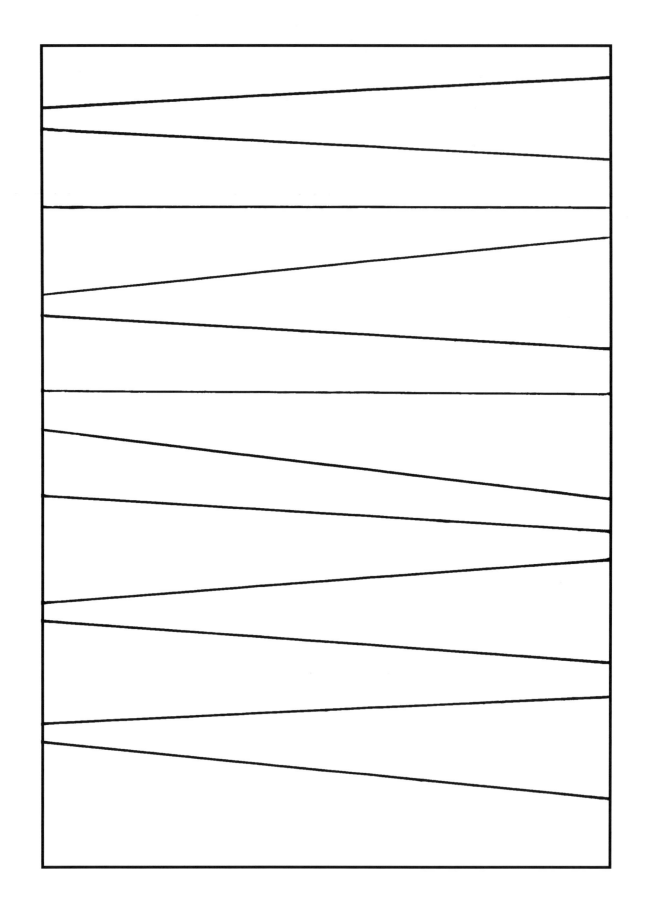

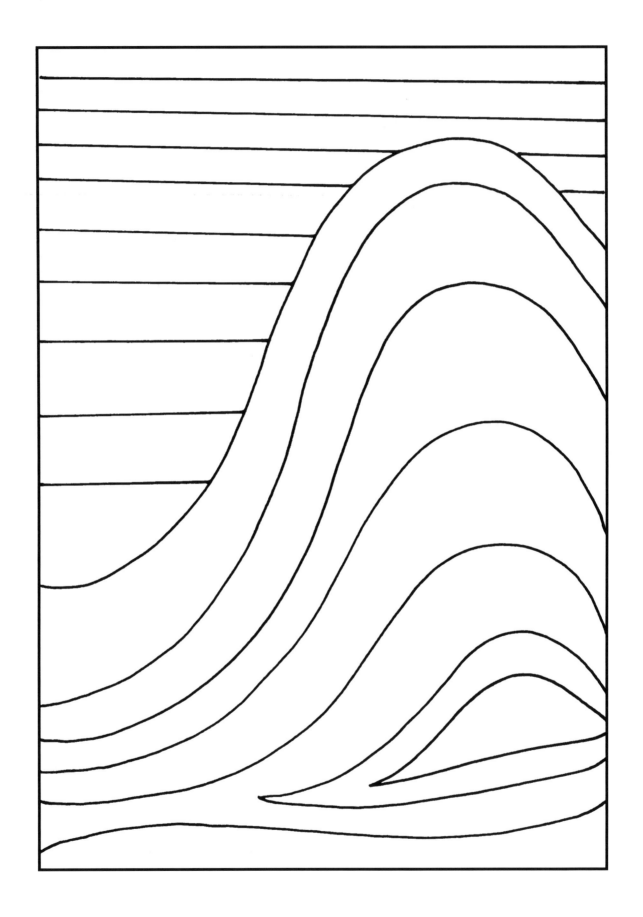

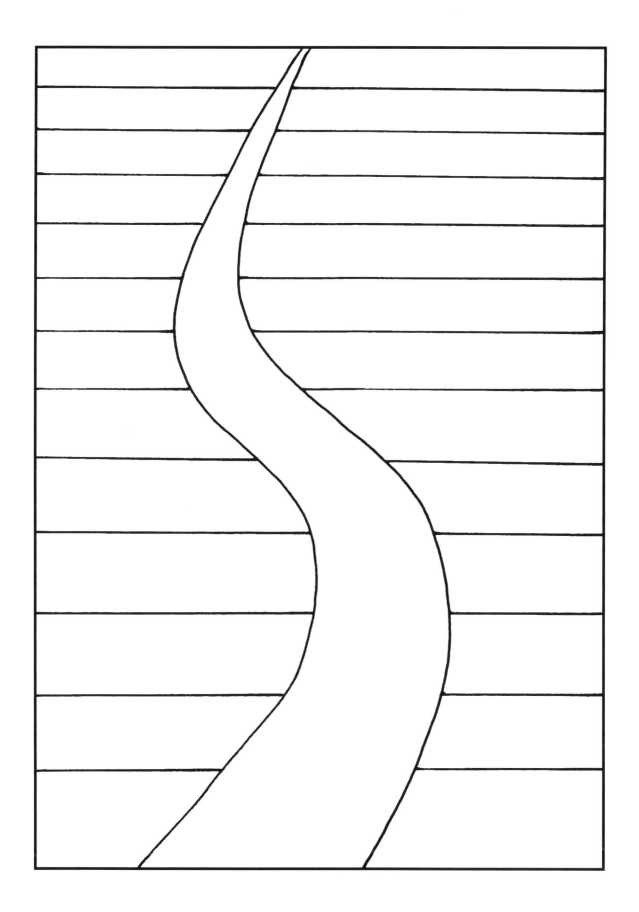

Digging Deeper Directions

By Denise Miller

1. Print or write out the verse or verses you want to dig deeper into (example on next page was printed with 2.5 spacing)

2. Look up different translations and see what words are different. Write out the different words over original wording or use arrows.

3. Add any additional information you find interesting. Ex: author, time period, where written, under what circumstances, to whom ... etc.

4. Follow anything you find interesting or that jumps out to you (Greek or Hebrew words, Commentaries, Strong's) ... add to your page or just soak it in.

5. Look up the accompanying references ... add to your page.

6. You can even add some sketchnotes or doodles if you like.

Digging deeper

Romans 12:1-2 ESV

Paul

plead
beseech
urge

those in Rome
loved by God

I appeal to you therefore, brothers, by

offer

the mercies of God, to present your

bodies as a living sacrifice, holy and

pleasing

acceptable to God, which is your

true & proper worship
offering ← spiritual worship. ² Do not be conformed
spiritual service

Copy, become, fashioned

1 Pet 1:14
As obedient
Children, do
not be
conformed
to the passions
of your
former Ignorance

NIV (pattern of)   age
to this world, but be transformed by the

renewing
renewal of your mind, that by testing

prove
learn
you may discern what is the will of God,

pleasing
what is good and acceptable and

perfect.

Digging Deeper

Tag Flap Book – Names of God
By Denise Miller

1		Purchase or make 5 tags (these are 3" x 6 1/4"... any size works) No hole needed
2	(Optional) Paint or decorate tags	
3	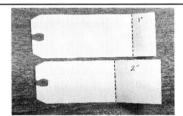	Fold first tag at 1", second tag at 2"... and so on
4	Stack tags lining up creases	
5		Stitch, sew or staple at crease
6	Write names along edge	
7	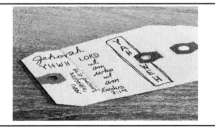	Write description of name, journal or draw on rest of flap

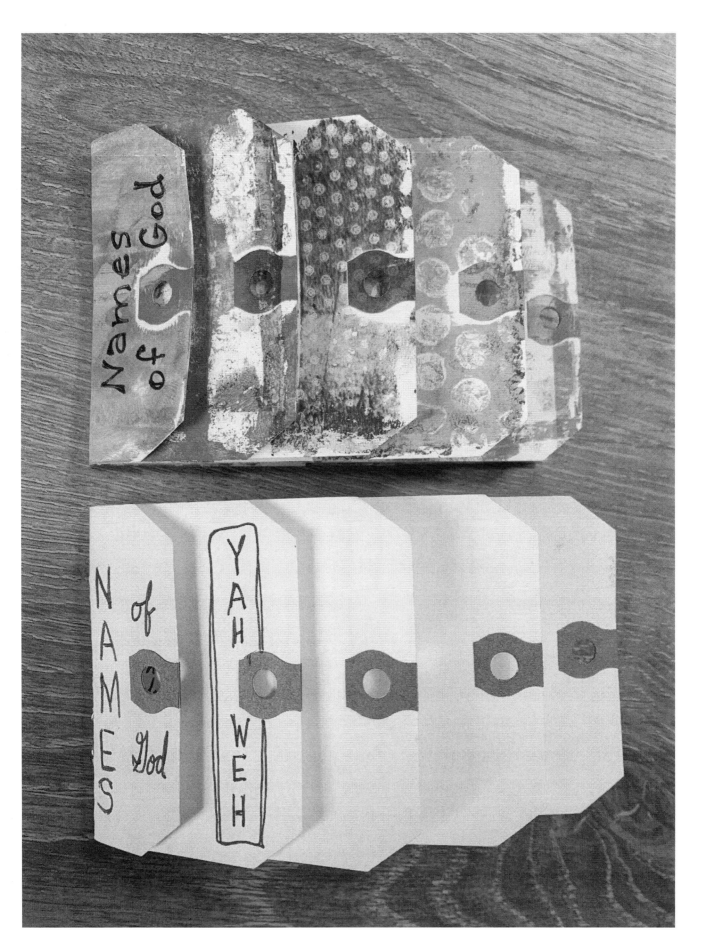

Conformed to Transformed

Mixed media is a very expressive art form. As you can see, both of these projects are very similar (directions) but the final layers are different. Take time to pray. Spend some time in God's word and the bible study. See where you think God is leading you, or if a verse resonates with you, use that verse. There is no wrong way to do this project.

May I Be Transformed
By Denise Miller

Conformed to Transformed
By Candice Schwark

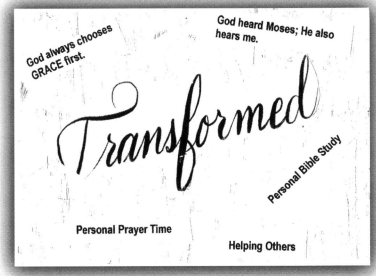

May I Be Transformed

By Denise Miller

Step 1. Journal on a page with any pencil, pen, or paint

+ What am I focusing on – have become my idols?

+ What have I conformed to?

+ What have I compromised on?

+ What have I ignored?

Step 2. Cover writing by scraping, painting, coloring, or collaging.

+ Use red to symbolize the blood of Jesus. He died for our sins.

+ Let page dry.

Step 3. Cover red layer with white paint or gesso.

+ The white symbolizes being washed clean.

Step 4. (optional) Add journaling. This can cover the whole page, part of it, or only in a small area.

+ What areas in my life have I been transformed in?

+ Write out a prayer.

+ Write out a praise.

Step 5. Add a statement, word, bible verse, declaration, or phrase.

+ Let this represent your hope of transformation.

+ Write BIG.

+ Use a marker, thick pen, paint, or printed from computer.

Examples of final layer wording:

+ TRANSFORMED

+ DEATH to LIFE

+ STANDING BOLDLY IN FAITH

+ MY SPIRITUAL WORSHIP

+ RENEWAL OF MY MIND

+ ACCEPTABLE TO GOD

Conformed to Transformed

by Candice Schwark

Sometimes we don't realize in our day-to-day actions how much we are conformed to the world. We accept things that are normal, when we know they really aren't. We sit in front of our computer, scrolling endlessly or playing games, when we know it's as mindless as watching television nonstop.

We need to regularly review our daily activities and measure the time spent on those worldly things against the amount of time dedicated to drawing closer to our Savior.

Try this technique:
* Using a sheet of paper that will take water-based products easily, write down those items in your day, month, or the past year that you have given to the world ... fallen into step with what others are saying or doing. Use any marker or pencil.

* Cover those words with red paint (using a brush, stiff card, marker) signifying the blood of Jesus shed for us. Write "Conformed" or paste word onto red paint - you can paste while the paint is wet and not use glue.

* We then remind ourselves that the blood of Jesus cleanses us - which we depict by covering the red with white Gesso or white paint until the red is covered. Some red showing is fine.

* Add "Transformed" from word page, or write "Conformed to Transformed" on the page, or a Bible verse, or a prayer, such as 'Jesus, I seek to follow your ways rather than my own."

* Add ways you can work on being transformed on top of the white paint: A couple of goals at a time is good. Next week, or month you can add some more goals, and/or check off some transformative actions that have become a consistent part of your life.

* Add from the word page or write "God always chooses grace first." and/or "As God heard Moses, so He also hears me."

This activity is a good way to review your life and how you are living it, and how you can be moved in a different direction, even in small increments. See how you did with the few goals you set.

Transformed

Transformed

Conformed

Conformed

Transformed

Transformed

Conformed

Conformed

Below: Choose as many as you want as immediate goal(s). Cut and paste or write them on your page. Add any others you like.

God always chooses GRACE first.

God heard Moses; He also hears me.

Bible Study in Fellowship

Church Fellowship

Be Still and Listen

Personal Devotional Time

Personal Prayer Time

Personal Bible Study

Helping Others

About Visual Faith™ Ministry

Visual Faith™ Ministry is the collaborative and creative work of online and in-person learning opportunities that enrich, encourage, and enable a wide variety of learning styles in order to tell the story of God's faithfulness in our lives and share the Gospel of Salvation through Jesus Christ.

Visual faith is all about reading, reflecting, and responding to God's Word. This might include writing, drawing, coloring, mixed media, or anything your imagination might devise to create consistent prayer and Bible Study habits in your walk with the Lord. Using visual faith tools and practices reminds us that we are made in the image of a creative God, and that our creative ideas or responses are a way to express our love to Him while we share Him with others.

Visual faith encourages and enables a daily time spent with the Lord as well as time spent sharing these experiences in community, at your church, or in your own home with family, neighbors, and friends. The value of time spent in these practices cannot be overstated. You will be blessed along with everyone who joins you or is the recipient of your efforts. In all of these ways and more, the practice of visual faith helps increase enjoyment of your relationship with God and gives you new ways to share Him creatively.

Visual Faith™ Ministry also offers over 2000 free resources, a Facebook community with over 2900 members to receive support and encouragement, Tuesdays@8 Livestream/Video resources on YouTube, and over 70 coaches, many of whom lead both in-person and online events throughout the country.

Find more Visual Faith™ Ministry resources at
visualfaithmin.org/shoppe

Questions? Please contact us at visualfaith@visualfaithmin.org

Join us online at:
Facebook @visualfaithmin
Instagram @visualfaithministry
Pinterest @visualfaithministry

Also from Visual Faith™ Ministries

The Movable Adventure Journal: A Visual Faith Companion to the Online Experience

VISUAL
FAITH™
MINISTRY

visualfaithmin.org

Made in the USA
Columbia, SC
07 January 2022

53839881R00083